P9-AGA-130

THE PRIMAL MIND

Also by Jamake Highwater

The Sun, He Dies (*novel*)

Anpao (*novel*)

Journey to the Sky: The Rediscovery of the Maya (*novel*)

Many Smokes, Many Moons: A Chronology of American
  Indian History Through Indian Art

Dance: Rituals of Experience

Ritual of the Wind: North American Indian Ceremonies,
  Music and Dances

Song from the Earth: American Indian Painting

Indian America: A Cultural and Travel Guide

The Sweet Grass Lives On: Fifty Contemporary
  North American Indian Artists

Masterpieces of American Indian Painting (*8 folios*)

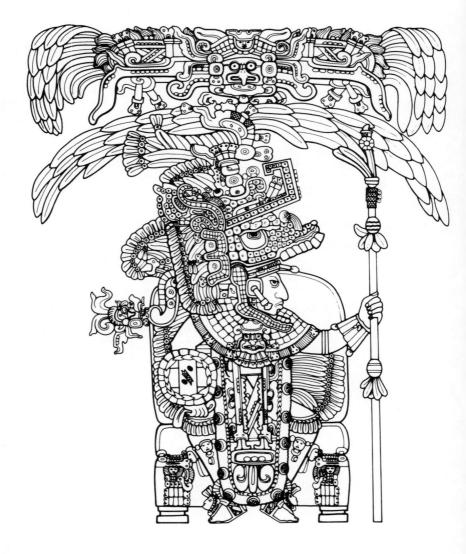

THE

PRIMAL

MIND

VISION AND REALITY
IN INDIAN AMERICA

Jamake Highwater

HARPER & ROW, PUBLISHERS, New York
Cambridge, Hagerstown, Philadelphia, San Francisco
1817 *London, Mexico City, São Paulo, Sydney*

The frontispiece is from a lintel of sapodilla wood from Temple IV at Tikal, Guatemala; Classic period, c. A.D. 747; Museum Für Völkerkunde, Basel.

The E. Honig translation of "Agosto/August" by Federico García Lorca on page 102 is reprinted by permission of Edwin Honig, © 1944.

FIRST EDITION

Designer: Sidney Feinberg

Library of Congress Cataloging in Publication Data

Highwater, Jamake.
  The primal mind.
  Bibliography: p.
  Includes index.
  1. Indians of North America—Philosophy,
2. Philosophy, Comparative. 3. Reality. I. Title.
E98.P5H53 1981   191'.08997   80-8929
ISBN 0-06-014866-7

---

81 82 83 84 85 10 9 8 7 6 5 4 3 2 1

To Guido Majno and Isabelle Joris
Sur la soudaineté de notre amitié . . .
—MALLARMÉ

CONTENTS

What sets worlds in motion is the interplay of differences, their attractions and repulsions. Life is plurality, death is uniformity. By suppressing differences and peculiarities, by eliminating different civilizations and cultures, progress weakens life and favors death. The ideal of a single civilization for everyone, implicit in the cult of progress and technique, impoverishes and mutilates us. Every view of the world that becomes extinct, every culture that disappears, diminishes a possibility of life.

—OCTAVIO PAZ (1967)

PRELUDE:
A CHERISHED ALIENATION

Why are you an art student?

Because art is the last door through which my parents think they can push me into the outer world.

—QUENTIN CRISP

This book contains a series of personal views that have come out of my experience in two widely separated cultures and lifestyles. That dual experience is likely to remain rare for a few more generations because we are never urged to attain anything but cultural single-mindedness. Some of us (and there are many more each generation) have stumbled into a newly forged sensibility made of irreconcilable values which, though never truly reconciled, have fused themselves into a new mentality. Because I wish to make a distinction between cultural assimilation with all its negative connotations and the kind of fusion about which I am writing here, I call this amalgamation of two unique ethnos *acculturation*. That process is the metaphor of this book.

I speak out of this dual cultural orientation rather than from the exclusive standpoint of any of the Western disciplines in which I was trained or any of the equally exclusive traditional Blackfeet values given to me by my mother and childhood teachers. My training in Western ideologies does not give me any special vantage. It is my educational *duplexity* in two completely contrary sets of values that gives impetus to what I have to say in this book.

The British physicist and philosopher L. L. Whyte has written that "thought is born of failure." When our actions are satisfying there is nothing left over to nag us. We are consumed by action, by process rather than contemplation. "To think is to confess a lack of adjustment which we must stop to consider. Only when the human organism fails to achieve an adequate response to its situation is there material for the processes of thought, and the greater the failure the more searching they become."

Indians and non-Indians are currently faced with a failure so vast that the basis of thought itself (the operation of thought itself) has come under close scrutiny. As I shall try to show in the opening chapters of *The Primal Mind*, both the Indian world and the world of Western civilization are confronted by immense spiritual and intellectual problems. Among primal peoples all over the world there is a sense of failure similar to that of those Native Americans who saw the massacre of a band of Ghost Dancers at Wounded Knee in 1890. Despite the protection of their Ghost Dance costumes, which the last Indian prophet Wovoka promised would make them invulnerable against the invaders' bullets, they were utterly destroyed. The Plains Indians' spiritual vision in which they might remain sovereign and free was demolished. Indians have never fully recovered a crucial aspect of their worldview since that terrible day at Wounded Knee.

A similar catastrophe overtook Western civilization as well, though its perpetrators were insiders rather than invaders. During the same decade of the late nineteenth century that saw the destruction of Native American spiritualism, the West was dealt a series of intellectual blows. The most essential Western conception, that of "progress," was almost nullified. And the fundamental spiritual values of the West were steadily undermined by science and philosophy. The vivid and aggressive Western belief in the certitude of reason (Logos), which had supported its sense of superiority since the time of Plato, was badly shaken.

As a result of a century-long intellectual revolution, the people of the West have lost hold of the Manifest Destiny which bloomed from their notion of themselves as a chosen people whom their god had predestined to dominate the cosmos. The rational basis for this ethnocentricity has long vanished, though, as we shall witness, its popular conviction is very slow in dying.

When a great ideal has ceased to illuminate the human values of a society and has lost its pervasive power as a system of beliefs, people have no choice but to search for something else with which to identify themselves. "At such moments," Whyte has said, "men may believe that they have lost something beyond price, for a grand vision has faded into despair and self-assurance given place to the humiliation of man's inability to understand himself. . . . Change cannot come until neither loyalty to the old nor fear of the new can longer delay it. Such a transformation is all the more difficult because it seems to require the greater to be exchanged for the less. Each real advance is paid for by aiming at less in order to achieve more. The crucial step cannot be taken until men are ready to choose the less which can be realized in place of the more which had remained a dream."

Thus there is a difference between being a cultural traditionalist and being a political reactionary. Tradition is big and strong enough to accommodate change; but for the reactionary mind change is both an evil and an impossibility.

In the last decades of the twentieth century we have come to realize that none of us can afford to be a chosen people. All our acts of atrocity have not brought us any closer to that terrible ethnocentric dream of superiority. Assimilation and genocide have not destroyed the "savages" despite the incomparable technology available to missionaries and exterminators. The age of empires has steadily collapsed and now the dominant culture is confronted by the undeniable fact that the "Melting Pot" equation in which it believed has turned out to be a self-serving fallacy. The "savages" have not only survived but multiplied and found their voices. Human diversity has not been vanquished by conformity and assimilation but has been magnified by our widening world perspective. What remains for all of us is a precious pluralism that is real—though it may seem to be less of a reality than we expected of the god or gods who promised each of us absolute dominion.

This book is an effort to speak out of that plurality of mentalities while at the same time illuminating the values and viewpoints of primal peoples whose ideas have been largely ignored by the dominant cultures. When I can do so, I will draw upon ideals and attitudes of the Indo-European intelligence (which is referred to in this book as *Western civilization*), because this method may help to clarify what I have to say about the primal mentality existing among peoples outside the Indo-European world. But my intention and plan for this book is never one of justifying or explaining away our crucial differences, for I intend, to the contrary, to celebrate those multitudes of things that make us distinctive and unique. I hope to convince those who live within a monopolistic mentality that "alienation" is a precious fact of life that has validity and gives vitality to thoughts born of our failure to be the *one* people we thought and hoped we were.

This affirmation of the many ideals of outsiders may serve those for whom alienation has been a terrible castigation rather than a gift, for whom it has been a blemish on some impossible Faustian dream of human conformity and spiritual unity. And this is how I hope to transform a generalization into a cultural metaphor. I believe that in the experience of the outsider there is an important lesson to be learned. But the virtues of this lesson are not accessible to those who can only see through one cultural window—one sexuality, one mentality, one reality. It demands more than sight to see. It requires vision. And vision, by the definitions of all the prophets, is the gift of those who stand in an ideal isolation . . . astronomers of those deepest spaces where we flash our desperate messages across the infinite space that separates us.

"These are singular people," the remarkable photographer Diane Arbus once said of her "models," "who appear like metaphors somewhere farther out than we do, beckoned, not driven, invented by belief, author and hero of a real dream by which our own courage and cunning are tested and tried; so that we may wonder all over again what is veritable and inevitable and possible and what it is to become whoever we may be."

I am exceedingly grateful to my editors Beatrice Rosenfeld and Cass Canfield, Jr. for their profound concern and interest, keen insights, and generous efforts in publishing this book. I also wish to thank Dr. Richard Thurn, who has shared so many formative ideas with me ever since our university days and during our numerous treks around the world. These essays were originally built, one by one over a period of five years, as a series of lectures given annually at the Medical Center of the University of Massachusetts in Worcester at the invitation of my friends Dr. Guido Majno and his colleague Dr. Isabelle Joris. It is with the greatest pleasure that I dedicate this book to these friends whose scholarship and humanism were fundamental to my inspiration.

The focus of *The Primal Mind* was much sharpened by the rousing debates and conversations of students and faculty members at Worcester. Eventually I took the same lectures to the Medical Center of the University of Oklahoma, to the University of Lethbridge in Alberta, Canada, and to many other institutions where I had the very good fortune of talking to and listening to Native American students and teachers concerned on a daily basis with interracial issues. Eventually I was invited by New York University to present "The

Primal Mind" as a seminar for the Continuing Adult Education Program. This lecture series prompted me to elaborate several years of talking, writing, and thinking about the essential and vital ways in which various peoples of the world differ from one another.

I am grateful to all of these people and institutions and to many other colleagues for their contributions to this book. Since my theme draws upon the most fundamental ideas of my lifetime, I cannot possibly give adequate credit to all the influences reflected in *The Primal Mind,* but perhaps the selected bibliography at the close of this book will help to highlight some of the major sources of ideas and opinions in my depiction of our pluralistic world.

Since my cultural background follows none of the easy stereotypes and since this series of personal essays grew out of my personal history, it might be a good idea to speak briefly about myself.

My mother, despite her complex blend of French Canadian and Blackfeet (Blood) ancestry, somehow retained much of the special *inclusivity* which I identify with the very heart of the primal world. She rarely expressed intolerance toward anything or anyone, and she was always capable of sustaining utter faith in the most contradictory realities—which is doubtlessly how she managed to keep alive her innermost identity as an Indian despite all the events that took her farther and farther from her origins.

Although my mother's mother and father apparently died of starvation and she and her sister were passed from one foster home to another, she was completely untouched by loathing for the self-righteousness of her various guardians and their evangelistic intentions. Though I suspect my mother had been christened she retained an unperturbable faith in her tribal realities, which she passed along to me in a

strong and constant voice. Her vivid teachings were my access to the Indian world, for I grew up constantly on the
move and never had the advantages of the extended family
life which mark the training of most primal peoples.

Though my mother could neither read nor write she spun
her recollections in Blackfeet and French and her faltering
English into a rare and enlightened acceptance of the world
and all the myriad ideals that preoccupy it. From my disin-
herited mother I learned to stay alive by dreaming myself
into existence—no matter how many forces attempted to ne-
gate or to confine my sense of identity and pride. From her I
learned that *everything* is real. It was a lesson of enormous
value to me, especially during these days of Indian national-
ism when the authenticity of urban Indians is constantly under scrutiny.

My father was not a traditional Indian. I am not even certain if both of his parents were Native people. He was a
renegade and an alcoholic—a marvelous, energetic man who
helped to organize the American Indian Rodeo Association
back in the 1940s. He called himself by many names during
his career in circuses, carnivals, and rodeos, but by the time
he met my then sixteen-year-old mother somewhere in the
American Northwest his name was Jamie Highwater. He
came from Virginia, Tennessee, or North Carolina, depending on his memory and his mood, and he knew very little
about his Eastern Cherokee heritage despite his intense
pride in being an Indian. He was a very dark, tall, and handsome man with great athletic abilities. Eventually he became
a rodeo clown and traveled around the endless pow-wow
circuits. Then producers on locations in Montana, Wyoming,
the Dakotas, and down in Arizona's Monument Valley began using my father as a stuntman in western films, which
prompted a new career and brought about much traveling
and extended visits to Southern California for my family.

Jamie Highwater died hundreds of times for John Wayne. Then, when I was about ten years old, he died for the last time in an automobile collision. I was adopted by my father's closest friend—a castabout, sometime actor in films, and ex-circus aerialist; and I spent my adolescence in his San Fernando Valley home and became "J Marks."

Since those difficult days of living between two cultures I have reclaimed my own name and I have also traveled the arduous journey back to my cultural identity. The grand climax of my professional and personal life took place on March 29, 1979 at Lethbridge University in Alberta, Canada, when Ed Calf Robe, Elder of the Blood Reserve of Blackfeet Indians, a member of the Horns Society, and a descendant of the famous chief Calf Robe, conferred a new name upon me to honor my achievements on behalf of my people. It is a ceremony usually reserved for a *minipoka*, "a favored child" of the Blackfeet Nation. My new name is Piitai Sahkomaapii, meaning "Eagle Son." This name-ceremony was the vindication of my mother's constant efforts to keep my heritage alive within me. Sadly, she had passed away and could not see the embrace of my people for which she had longed all her life.

The Indian world is not easy. Subjugation has taught us too much about the limits of human tolerance and we ourselves have become more than a bit exclusive, bitter, and defensive. But beneath the inevitable outrage of those who have been abused there still shines in Indians a primal mentality which is fundamentally inclusive and which accepts rather than rejects. That inclusivity, that affirmation of life is what I learned from the lessons of my mother, and these values are the ultimate subjects of this book.

—JAMAKE HIGHWATER
Piitai Sahkomaapii
New York City, 1980

NOTE: In view of the purposes of this book the term "primitive" has been changed to [primal] in all quoted materials except when the quoted authors clearly mean to imply "savage" or "rude and wild." It is pointless to perpetuate an offensive term or to quote authors whose ideas about aboriginal peoples are quite the opposite of what is implied today by the term "primitive." We assume that various uses of the word "primitive" came about because previously there was no alternative word in general use and authors were not aware of the emphatic need to abandon an offensive term like "primitive."

Attribution for all materials quoted in this book may be found in the selective bibliography under the author's name. If there is more than one book or article listed for a given author, then the date of the publication of the work from which a quotation is drawn is listed parenthetically after the name of the author each time it appears in the text: i.e., Susanne Langer (1957), etc.

I

INTRODUCING THE PRIMAL MIND

1

THE INTELLECTUAL
SAVAGE

> Our most stubborn and pertinacious assumptions are precisely those which remain unconscious and therefore uncritical, concepts like creative imagination or expressive communication, and others which we take for granted without realizing that we do so, their pristine novelty and vigor eroded by the platitudinous complacency of middle age. The best and perhaps the only sure way of bringing to light and revivifying these fossilized assumptions, and of destroying their power to cramp and confine, is by subjecting ourselves to the shock of contact with a very alien tradition.
> —HAROLD OSBORNE

The greatest distance between people is not space but culture.

When I was a child I began the arduous tasks of exploring the infinite distance between peoples and building bridges that might provide me with a grasp of the mentality of Native Americans as it relates to the worldview of other civilizations. I had to undertake this task in order to save my life; for had I simply accepted the conventions by which white people look at themselves and their world I would have lost the interior visions that make me an Indian, an artist, and an individual.

This perilous exploration of reality began for me in southern Alberta and in the Rockies of Montana when I was about five years old. One day I discovered a wonderful creature. It looked like a bird, but it was able to do things that many other birds cannot do. For instance, in addition to flying in the enormous sky, it swam and dove in the lakes and, sometimes, it just floated majestically on the water's silver surface. It would also waddle rather gracelessly in the tall grasses that grew along the shores. That bird was called *méksikatsi*, which, in the Blackfeet language, means "pink-colored feet." Méksikatsi seemed an ideal name for the versatile fly-swim bird, since it really did have bright pink feet.

When I was about ten years old my life changed abruptly and drastically. I was placed in an orphanage because my parents were destitute, and eventually I was adopted by a non-Indian foster father when my own parent was killed in an automobile accident. I found myself wrenched out of the world that was familiar to me and plunged without guidance into an entirely alien existence. I was told to forget my origins and try to become somebody I was not.

One day a teacher of English told me that méksikatsi was not really méksikatsi. It didn't matter that the word described the bird exactly for me or that the Blackfeet people had called it méksikatsi for thousands of years. The bird, I was told, was called duck.

"DUCK?"

Well, I was extremely disappointed with the English language. The word "duck" didn't make any sense, for indeed méksikatsi doesn't look like the word "duck." It doesn't even sound like the word "duck." And what made the situation all the more troublesome was the realization that the English verb "to duck" was derived from the actions of the bird and not vice versa. So why do people call méksikatsi *duck*?

This lesson was the first of many from which I slowly learned, to my amazement, that the people of white America don't *see* the same things that Indians see.

As my education in the ways of non-Indian people progressed, I finally came to understand what duck means to them—but I could never forget that méksikatsi also has meaning, even though it means something fundamentally different from what duck means.

This lesson in words and the ideas they convey is very difficult to understand, especially if we grow up insulated by a single culture and its single language. In fact, it has been the most complicated lesson of my life. As I have gained experience and education in both the dominant culture and that of Indians, I have found it progressively more difficult to pass from one world to the other. I had to discover a place somewhere between two worlds. It is not simply a matter of language, for, as everyone knows, it is possible to translate with fair accuracy from one language to another without losing too much of the original meaning. But there are no methods by which we can translate a mentality and its alien ideas.

I am very much alienated by the way some ideas find their way into English words. For instance, when an English word is descriptive—like the word "wilderness"—I am often appalled by what is implied by the description. After all, the forest is not "wild" in the sense that it is something needing to be tamed or controlled and harnessed. For Blackfeet Indians, the forest is the natural state of the world. It is the cities that are wild and seem to need "taming." For most primal peoples the earth is so marvelous that their connotation of it requires it to be spelled in English with a capital "E." How perplexing it is to discover two English synonyms for Earth—"soil" and "dirt"—used to describe uncleanliness, *soiled* and *dirty*. And how upsetting it is to discover that the word "dirty" in English is also used to depict obscenities! Or take the English word "universe," in which I find even more complicated problems, for Indians do not believe in a *"uni-*verse," but in a *"multi-*verse." Indians don't believe that there is *one* fixed and eternal truth; they think there are many different and equally valid truths.

The late Hannah Arendt has given a vivid depiction of this concept of Indian reality, though she did not intend to clarify anything but the multifaceted nature of reality itself. She said in her last book, *The Life of the Mind*, that the impulse behind the use of reason is not the discovery of truth but the discovery of meaning—and that truth and meaning are not the same things.

If we can accept the paradox that the real humanity of people is understood through cultural differences rather than cultural similarities, then we can make profound sense of our differences. It is possible that there is not one truth, but many; not one real experience, but many realities; not one history, but many different and valid ways of looking at events.

At the core of each person's life is a package of beliefs that he or she learns and that has been culturally determined long in advance of the person's birth. That is equally true for Indians and for white people. The world is made coherent by our description of it. Language permits us to express ourselves, but it also places limits on what we are able to say. What we call things largely determines how we evaluate them. What we see when we speak of "reality" is simply that preconception—that cultural package we inherited at birth. For me it was méksikatsi; for an English-speaking child it was duck.

Indian children have long been urged by educators to see things and to name them in terms of the cultural package of white people, though such training essentially divests Indians of their unique grasp of reality, of their own dissimilar cultural package. Children of the dominant society are rarely given the opportunity to know the world as others know it. Therefore they come to believe that there is only one world, one reality, one truth—the one they personally know; and they are inclined to dismiss all other worlds as illusions.

Evidence that Indians have a different manner of looking at the world can be found in the contrast between the ways in which Indian and non-Indian artists depict the same events. That difference is not necessarily a matter of "error" or simply a variation in imagery. It represents an entirely individual way of seeing the world. For instance, in a sixteenth-century anonymous engraving of a famous scene from the white man's history an artist depicted a sailing vessel anchored offshore with a landing party of elegantly dressed gentlemen disembarking while regal, Europeanized Indians look on—one carrying a "peace pipe" expressly for this festive occasion.

The drawing by an Indian, on the other hand, records a totally different scene: Indians gasping in amazement as a floating island, covered with tall defoliated trees and odd creatures with hairy faces, approaches.

When I showed the two pictures to white people they said in effect: "Well, of course you realize that what those Indians thought they saw was not really there. They were unfamiliar with what was happening to them and so they misunderstood their experience." In other words, there were no defoliated trees, no floating island, but a ship with a party of explorers.

Indians, looking at the same pictures, pause with perplexity and then say, "Well, after all, a ship is a floating island, and what really are the masts of a ship but the trunks of tall trees?" In other words, what the Indians saw was real in terms of their own experience.

The Indians saw a floating island while white people saw a ship. Isn't it also possible—if we use the bounds of twentieth-century imagination—that another, more alien people with an utterly different way of seeing and thinking might see neither an island nor a ship? They might for example see the complex networks of molecules that physics tells us produce the outward shapes, colors, and textures that we simply *see* as objects. Albert Einstein showed us that objects, as well as scientific observation of them, are not experienced directly, and that common-sense thinking is a kind of shorthand that attempts to convert the fluid, sensuous animation and immediacy of the world into illusory constructs such as stones, trees, ships, and stars.

We see the world in terms of our cultural heritage and the capacity of our perceptual organs to deliver culturally predetermined messages to us. We possess no closer, no less fallible hold on reality. Yet among politically concerned people there is a good-natured insistence that all peoples are fundamentally the same. Some libertarians seem to believe that even biology is democratic, but what they see when they refer to the homogeneous attributes of all human physiology is not blood or nerve cells, but things much more culutural. They do not like to notice that races and national groups tend to evolve distinctive stereotypes emotionally and physically. They believe that all people are fundamentally the same because all people—they insist—need and want the same things. They do not take into consideration, for example, the reason a Navajo family may rip the toilet out of its newly built government house. Traditional Navajos believe it is disgusting to put a toilet under the roof of their living quarters rather than at a distance from the dwelling place. People come away from the Navajo Reservation expressing their sorrow in finding that "the poor Indians do not have indoor plumbing and live in terrible, primitive conditions unfit for human beings." But their concern is misplaced, as they would realize if they knew a bit more about Navajo tribal attitudes. What they have done is to confuse tradition with squalor. They come away feeling sorry for people simply because those people don't possess the things they themselves need and want out of life.

Liberal people have been polarized by the atrocities and inequities of history—especially the incredible cruelties of our own times. They want to do away with human misery even if it means the destruction of the realities of other cultures. What they fail to take into account is the great variety of ways in which the members of a single culture respond to the same things, let alone the vaster differences that exist between cultures. There is no question that all people feel sorrow and happiness, but the things that evoke these responses and the manner in which such feelings may be expressed socially and privately can be highly dissimilar from culture to culture. The Mexican poet and scholar Octavio Paz (1967) has stated: "The ideal of a single civilization for everyone, implicit in the cult of progress and technique, impoverishes and mutilates us."

Political idealists have overemphasized the uniformity of people in their efforts to destroy intolerance. It is exceedingly dangerous to take democratic idealism out of politics and attempt to apply it to psychology, science, and art. The uniformity that biologists and physicists discover at the core of the material world is tenuous at best and is easily distorted into conformity when applied to less fundamental issues, and gradually we find that the very democratic process that is supposed to set us free has deprived cultures and individuals of the right to be dissimilar.

For many decades it was unfashionable to suggest that all people are not the same. It was equally unpopular to insist that we can learn more about a culture from its differences than from its similarities to other cultures, and that the basis of human nature is probably more visible in human diversity than through the relatively few ways in which we are really and fundamentally the same. Liberals have striven for admirable but somewhat naive political goals: one nation, one world, one equation by which everything and everybody can be understood. In the process of trying to unify the world we must be exceedingly careful not to destroy the diversity of the many cultures of humankind that give our lives meaning, focus, vision, and vitality.

For a long time the viewpoints of primal peoples, such as the Indians of the Americas, were considered naive and primitive, especially if the peoples kept their history alive through oral and pictorial traditions rather than by writing history books. Today we are learning that people are not the same, and that we cannot evaluate all experience in the same way. We are also learning that everybody doesn't have to be the same in order to be equal. It is no longer realistic for dominant cultures to send out missionaries to convert everyone to their singular ideas of the "truth." Today we are beginning to look into the ideas of groups outside the dominant culture; we are finding different kinds of "truth" that make the world we live in far bigger than we dreamed it could be.

"Psychological differences exist between all nations and races," Carl Jung insisted—though his concepts of human archetypes have been repeatedly used to claim the contrary. "There are in fact differences between families and individuals. That is why I attack every leveling psychology when it raises a claim to *universal* validity. All leveling produces hatred and venom in the suppressed and it prevents any broad human understanding. All branches of mankind unite in one trunk, yes! . . . but what is a tree without its many separate branches?"

The conception of the one, the absolute, has dominated the mentality of a long succession of technological civilizations. The monopolistic, monotheistic mandate has largely deprived all but primal peoples of a grasp of "the other." Perhaps this capacity for vision was lost in the West long ago when the makers of great sagas and the painters of sacred images in caves passed out of existence. Perhaps in primal people like American Indians there survives a precious reservoir of humanity's visionary power. Antonio Machado-Ruiz, the Spanish poet and scholar, came to the same conclusions, though his perspective was Western and he therefore saw our diversity as an incurable but marvelous affliction.

"The *other* does not exist: this is the conclusion of rational faith, the incurable belief of human reason. Identity equals Reality . . . as if, in the end, everything must necessarily and absolutely be *one and the same*. But the *other* refuses to disappear; it subsists, it persists; it is the hard bone on which reason breaks its teeth." With a poetic faith as human as rational faith, Machado-Ruiz believed in the other, in "the essential Heterogeneity of being," in what might be called "the inscrutable *otherness* from which oneness must always suffer."

The exploration of this otherness began for me in northern Montana when I was a child. I was born in the twilight of Western monopolism. Like many young, nearly assimilated primal people all over the world, I became for the first time conscious of the "intelligence" at work in my own culture. I ceased being ashamed of it and I ceased trying to justify it. I became aware of the potential of vivifying my heritage rather than sacrificing it. Of course there were many isolated and brave Indian spokespersons in the past,* but mine was the first generation for whom the use of the Western type of intelligence became a pervasive tool rather than a vehicle for assimilation and ethnic suicide. During the early decades of this century, private and parochial organizations and the federal government sponsored massive Indian educational efforts, often involving boarding schools. As the Oglala Sioux writer Michael Taylor has pointed out: "Disruptive of ordinary tribal life and sometimes brutal and insensitive to human needs, the schools notably failed in their initial purpose of eradicating native languages, religions,

---

* Among the important Indian spokespersons in the past were such leaders and writers as Thayendanegea (Joseph Bran, 1742-1809); Tecumtha (Tecumseh, 1768-1813); Pontiac (1720-69); Keokuk (1780-1848); Aleek-chea-ahoosh (Plenty Coups, 1848-1932); Highn'moot Tooyalakekt (Chief Joseph, 1840-1904); Ohiyesa (Charles Eastman, 1848-1939); and many other outstanding Native people.

and customs. What the schools did accomplish, accidentally, was to provide Indian people from divergent backgrounds with a means of communication—the English language."

With our skills in the language of the dominant culture came significant insights about who "we" are and who "they" are. Social changes greatly facilitated our efforts to become educated fully in the cultures of two different worlds without giving up any important aspect of our own cultural and individual identities. My generation was the first to attend in great numbers both the ritual "schools" of our own cultures and the higher institutions of the white world. We grew up in two Americas—the ancient one that had existed for our ancestors for tens of thousands of years and the new one that is written about in history books. The tales of those two Americas are rarely compatible—and we quickly came to grasp our perilous situation. We had to make convincing use of our newly acquired intellectual skills in order to sustain our primal culture. We had to re- lease a tide of communication between two worlds, and to do this we had to be a kind of people who had never before existed. We had to abandon both Andrew Jackson's *Wild In- dians* and Jean-Jacques Rousseau's *Noble Savage* and emerge as a new cultural mutant—the *Intellectual Savage*—who was capable of surviving equally in two worlds by tenaciously retaining the ritual apparatus of primal people at the same time that we were attaining the intellectual and communica- tions paraphernalia of the dominant societies.

It is through the visionary apprehension of "the other" that we attain each other. Without a grasp of the *essential het- erogeneity of being* we commit ourselves to solitary confine- ment. All the education and refinement in the world cannot supplant a capacity for otherness. There can be nothing more horrifying for the victors of the Western world than to discover that they have won everything and in the process lost themselves. By methodically divesting their children of the capacity for vision they have forfeited the ability to see anybody but themselves.

✳ Among the languages of American Indians there is no word for "art." For Indians everything is art ... therefore it needs no name. My efforts, however, to find communicative accesses between the Native American world and the world of the dominant society convinced me that the metaphoric form of expression called "art" in the West is the best means of transcending the isolation of vastly dissimilar cultures. Curiously, this very important artistic connection can never be factual—for ultimately facts do not inform us. No matter how well informed a spectator may be on the techniques of the arts or the many aspects of an alien culture, if someone does not experience an aesthetic relationship to what is before him or her, all the information and education will not permit that person to cross the distance that exists between different peoples and, for that matter, between different individuals of the same technological society.

Art puts us in touch with "the other." Without art we are alone.

For me, art gradually became the essential bridge between my cultural, my individual alienation and the great world community, but the viability of that bridge depends upon what philosopher F.S.C. Northrop has called an aesthetic component, an attribute that is curiously lost among nonprimal peoples of both the West and the East.

Wherever the world is understood exclusively in terms of discursive facts there can be no access to other worlds. The poet René Char has said: "For those who are walled up everything is a wall ... even an open door." The vistas of all the great windows of walled-up cultures are simply mirrors. We see the world in terms of ourselves. Therefore when discussing the cosmos of the Indians of the Americas I inevitably find myself trying to open windows. To do this I must talk about art.

Artists all over the world have always known that art is fundamentally a way of *seeing*. Art, like matter-of-fact reality, has a real existence within all of us even though it seems to exist in the imaginal world. Artists are among the very few people in Western civilizations who have been permitted to deal with this visionary reality as something tangible and significant. The techniques and styles created by artists are not invented in order to be "original," but contrarily, they are the means by which they achieve something almost impossible: to provide for others the personal visions they have as artists.

In the dominant society people are asked to rely as little as possible on individual vision. In fact, if we rely too heavily upon it and depart too much from our acceptable cultural framework we are likely to be regarded as peculiar or dangerous. We may be considered dangerous because our experiences do not parallel those of our peers. Only the contemporary artist is allowed to look at the world in terms of an individual vision rather than in terms of his or her "cultural eye."

Though I would prefer to speak of primal mentality strictly in terms of the attitudes and cultures of American Indians, the primal mind has too recently become aware of itself and cannot yet, and perhaps by nature never will be able to, vivify itself in terms that are both its own and intelligible to non-Indians. Therefore I have attempted, during the years since I first learned that méksikatsi is "really" duck, to evolve a set of metaphors out of Western mentality that conveys something of the fundamental otherness of Indians. Of course this is exactly what Carlos Castaneda achieved in his cycle of Don Juan parables—a literature strikingly similar to the parables of Jesus and equally subject to the harsh Pauline "realism" of interpreters. Castaneda's work may not be truthful but it is meaningful, and that is ultimately what counts about any work of art or any philosophy.

Since I must employ metaphors evolved out of Western mentality, it is inevitable that my discussions of the primal mind will invoke contrasts and comparisons between discursive Western mentality and the aesthetic component that is at the core of the primal mind. Such contrasts and comparisons tend to polarize people, making them feel either attacked or excluded, because all of us tend to think of comparisons as judgmental. It remains, however, that I would not have grasped what Anglo-Americans mean by the words "duck" and "universe" if I had not attained a fundamental understanding of how these terms compare and contrast with Blackfeet words. Comparisons are inevitable and so too is the important cultural bias that all of us foster as part of our heritage.

In the broadest sense, the primal mind is a point of departure for a much larger idea. It is a metaphor for a type of otherness that parallels the experience of many people born into the dominant society who feel intensely uncomfortable and alien. It is this condition of alienation during the last decades of the twentieth century that has motivated this book. There is "an alien" in all of us. There is an artist in all of us. Of this there is simply no question. The existence of a visionary aspect in every person is the basis for the supreme impact and pervasiveness of art. Art is a staple of humanity. It can serve as a class distinction but it does so unwittingly. In fact, art has fundamentally the opposite relation to society insofar as it can function for any economic, intellectual, or social group. Art is so urgent, so utterly linked with the pulse of feeling in people, that it becomes the singular sign of life when every other aspect of civilization fails: in concentration camps, among the brutalized and the dispossessed, the mad and the too mighty. The people of the caves of Altamira built scaffolds in the dark interiors of their rock caverns, and with pigments made from ground roots and bark and minerals they painted an amazing world upon their ceilings by the meager light of oil lamps. They were spending their time drawing pictures when some would say that they should have been out finding food and facing the tremendous improbabilities of their survival. American Indian life perpetuates the primary idealism of those uncommonly common people who scaled scaffolds to invest the rocks with their story: their myths, their histories, their totems. That peculiar act of expression (which has only recently become known to us as art) makes visible much of the unique sensibility of primal people.

By associating the primal mind with an innate art impulse in humanity, I am talking not simply about American Indians, for whom this impulse is the entire life force, but about everyone in whom the marvelously ordinary capacity for vision survives.

"The point to be noted here," the American philosopher F.S.C. Northrop (1966) has written, "is not that art of this traditional Western type and theoretical knowledge of this Western kind are not the most excellent of art and knowledge of their kind, but merely that they are but one type of art and but one type of knowledge." There is an equally important and significant kind of experience that Northrop champions. It is the visionary, the aesthetic vantage point, which provides genuine knowledge in its own right. And it is specifically this illusive and alternative kind of knowledge that finds its creative source in the primal mind.

2

A SAVAGE LOOK
AT CIVILIZATION:

Lessons of the Cave, Lessons of the Earthquake

> Science is and always has been that admirable, active, ingenious, and bold way of thinking whose fundamental bias is to treat everything as though it were an object-in-general . . . as though it meant nothing to us and yet was predestined for our own use.
>
> —MAURICE MERLEAU-PONTY (1964d)

In the nineteenth centry, an English naturalist with a penchant for proving the insights of others caught sight of a ferocious, hideous, and fanged gorilla among the shadows and debris of human history. The naturalist was named Charles Darwin, and he believed that he could vaguely recognize in this terrible and obsolete manlike ape the distant cousin of *Homo sapiens*. His theories, as we know, revolutionized Western mentality and were central to the upheaval that has typified the twentieth-century's biological frame of reference. Curiously, primal people did not need the theories of Charles Darwin to convince them that humankind is an integral part of nature.

Raymond Dart, a later pioneer who in the 1920s unearthed evidence of ancient ape-men he called *Australopithecines*, regarded them as successful carnivores and killers of big game, club-swinging beasts, already capable of balancing on two feet, and the absolute terror of everything within their reach. Dart's image of primordial humanity set the pervasive stereotype for the subsequent generations of scientists and lay people. He considered these ape-men to be brutal and highly aggressive primates of very low mentality, capable of killing their own offspring, and carrying in their genes an implacable cruelty, sadism, and bloodthirstiness that came to be the quintessential opposite of the Victorian concept of what civilization represents.

An examination of Western anthropology and archaeology reveals the numerous ways in which Western people have conceived of themselves in relation to other peoples and how they have devised an image of progress placing themselves at the pinnacle of creation. This viewpoint has had a very important impact upon the dominant culture's evaluation of the various "pagans" and "barbarians" encountered during wide-flung explorations beyond the very narrow boundaries of its European homelands. Scientist Loren Eiseley has made a valuable observation: "The biologist of that day, lacking enough fossils to substantiate his points, sought to thrust living men and living animals closer together than the facts sometimes warranted. He aimed to animalize' man even if it required him to humanize the animal world which had previously been regarded as entirely remote from mankind." This was not a conscious attempt at deception, but a result of a particular Western intellectual climate—a tendency to see human evolution in terms of the eighteenth-century scale of nature.

In this way, the biologist could begin with one of the existing great apes—the gorilla, orang, or chimpanzee—as representing the earliest human stage of evolution, and from this erroneous supposition, pass to the existing races of humankind, which were arranged in a strictly vertical series of developments, with the white Victorian male assumed to represent the summit of the human evolutionary ascent. The fact that the existing apes are creatures contemporaneous with ourselves, who have evolved down an entirely different evolutionary pathway that is as highly specialized as our own, was not understood or taken into consideration by scholars of the nineteenth century. "Even the contemporary races of man," Eiseley has noted, "came to be regarded as living fossils. The past, so to speak, had been quietly transported into the present—assigned to living actors without their consent."

This consensus established a highly ethnocentric anthropological error: the farther back in the "ancestral cave" you live the more "primitive" you are and, therefore, the more lowly by comparison to the white male who places himself at the crown of creation. It is immediately clear how readily this error has served the political and economic aggressiveness of the West.

Though this theory of evolution has been abandoned in most professional circles, it persists as a prevalent conviction of lay people and is so subtly and deeply rooted in an unconscious racism that it ideally condones the tendency in the West to measure all things by the very high regard the dominant world has of itself. On the basis of the misconception of the ancestral cave, a repulsive equation has been formulated: the more that you "look like an ape" in color, facial structure, or other traits, the more "primitive" you are assumed to be; the more your pictorial traditions and material culture resemble the culture of so-called cavemen, the less civilized you are and the more lost in the eternal childhood of the "savage."

So much is revealed about the contrasting worldviews of primal and Western peoples in this history of evolutionary concepts—how various cultures see themselves in relation to the wholeness of nature—that I think it is valuable to explore the subject in some detail.

THE WESTERN MONOPOLY

Before we can build a bridge that spans the longest distance between peoples we must first construct sturdy abutments in both cultures, for bridges cannot be built—as we have often attempted to build them in the political arena— from only one side of the chasms we hope to span. And cultures cannot be understood from the perspectives of an "objective" science, because comparisons are inevitably made with the value judgments of a single outside culture. What is needed is an overview that possesses the discursive perspective as well as the visionary imagination of *both* cultures involved in the comparison. Clearly, information and statistics are not enough. Good will is not enough. And objectivity counts for nothing since it is, to begin with, an exclusively Western notion.

Yet, it should be admitted from the outset, ethnocentricity is not something in which only Western people engage. Most groups believe their view of things to be an exclusive kind of reality. Therefore we are all prone to make evaluations without employing any of the ideas and visions of the things we are attempting to evaluate. While we claim to be looking at someone else, we are always looking at ourselves.

A nonchalant sense of superiority toward outsiders is inevitable from such an approach to observation and social research. I am thinking, specifically, of a renowned contemporary book by a respected anthropologist that is subtitled: "The history of the various and often curious ways in which *the human race* has conceived of its own origins, nature and destiny." The book is not concerned with the conceptions held by the diverse peoples of the world—"the human race"—but is devoted entirely to European and American attitudes and theories. So subtly ethnocentric is the training of people in the dominant society that we would not usually notice the presumption of this subtitle, which amounts to the obliteration of primal peoples without even an apology for excluding them from the human race.

Western people are surely not alone in this self-serving racial malady. As we have already noted, many other groups also consider themselves to be chosen people. And even where there is less inclination to appoint one's own people as the special creatures of God, there is a tendency to identify one's own group as "the people" or "human beings." The salient point to be made about Western mentality, however, is that it has meticulously built an entire system of values and judgments upon the assumption that the people of the West are superior to everyone else; and this very dubious science of race has been supported by something called *objectivity* in which Western people believe without reservation. This conception of Native Americans, specifically, reveals the enormity of the dogma that must be overcome before we can possibly describe the primal mind in terms of itself.

SHADOWS OF FORGOTTEN ANCESTORS

When Giambattista Vico died in 1744 he left a unique legacy, the exceptional idea that society is manmade: "The world of civil society has certainly been made by men, and its principles are therefore to be found within the modifications of our own human minds." Vico believed that whereas the physical laws of the universe are stable, societies are constantly changing, and he made it his life's work to discover the laws governing social change.

In order to penetrate the "perennial springs of change," Vico began his investigation with "remote and obscure periods of history." Taking into account the scant and very dubious ethnographic literature of his day, he was among the first thinkers to regard primal peoples as full members of the human race and of social tradition. His Christian bias required him to give full credence to the biblical Genesis, but his uncommonly liberal mentality soon departed from orthodoxy to the degree it was possible in his time. According to Vico, some of Noah's unruly sons wandered away after the Flood and eventually forgot all vestiges of their Judaic culture—losing even the capacity for language and descending "to the level of wild beasts." Startled by great thunderclaps in the first mornings of the world, Vico's "savages" sought shelter in caves, and from there the European conception of the history of cultural evolution began. The descendants of Noah's cultivated sons rose quickly to become the founders of vast Western civilizations while Noah's regressive offspring became stereotypical *primitives* who "forcibly seized their women, who were naturally shy and unruly, dragged them into their caves, and, in order to have intercourse with them, keeping them there as perpetual lifelong companions. Thus . . . they gave a beginning to matrimony."

Though it is unclear who originated this unsavory and false image of primal peoples, and though this viewpoint has been much debated and revised, it is this ancient image that nonetheless persists and has been the consensus of so-called *primitives* since the time of Giambattista Vico.

The French political economist Anne-Robert-Jacques Turgot (1727–81) provided another conspicuous stereotype that we have come to associate with early humans and that helps to explain the Western depreciation of primal peoples. Turgot regarded leisure as an essential factor in the evolution of culture. And he concluded that the constant search for food by early nomadic hunters and cave dwellers left no time for creative activities. Civilization, according to Turgot, was facilitated by the invention of agriculture and the domestication of animals, providing an increased food supply and producing leisure time for the elite, who built houses, designed temples, and contrived writing and music. In this way Turgot firmly believed in *progress* and considered it to be the most important single factor in the evolution of humankind.

We cannot, however, give him credit or blame for the widespread contention that evolution is unalterably progressive, for that dubious distinction must be given to Marie Jean de Condorcet (1743–94), Turgot's close friend and biographer.

Far more enthusiastic about progress than Turgot, Condorcet elevated it to a state of utopian fulfillment. He believed that humanity is absolutely perfectible, and can never retrogress. "Nature has fixed no limits on our hopes," he stated in anticipation of the political and economic laissez faire of Adam Smith's *Wealth of Nations*. Thus, according to Condorcet, with time would automatically come immense, unending improvement in the human situation. Progress was propelled by its own power. It moved forward with or without human collaboration, leading humanity inevitably in the right direction along a narrow, vertical path that all the races and peoples of the world were required to tread in their universal ascension to the utopian state intended for humankind alone among all the things in creation.

Condorcet's highly secular conception of progress was therefore a beginning of the notion that we can judge a people's evolutionary status by its relationship to the achievements of Western civilization. His views of progress reiterate the idea that only one cultural path leads out of the ancestral cave, and therefore all peoples must progress through the exact same evolutionary stages in a prescribed succession of steps if they are to attain what the West calls maturity and high civilization. All cultural activity outside this vertical pattern of progress is therefore seen as a perpetual backwater. These notions are implicit in the exclusively Western idea of progress, which is one of the most basic presumptions of the mentality of the West.

THE CAVE AS A RACIAL PRISON

The popular consensus of evolution and progress that prevails today derives largely from these first, stumbling conceptions of the origin, character, and destiny of humanity.

The work of one eighteenth-century scholar of evolution reinforced this conviction. Charles de Brosses (1709–77) was concerned with animal worship, as practiced among Egyptians, and was so utterly repulsed by the customs he discovered beyond the boundaries of Europe that he explained them as fictions of debilitated, savage minds. It was de Brosses who invented the term "Fetishism" to describe such primal, animal objects of worship. He gave particular emphasis to a picture of early humankind as irrational, as "barbarous and necessitous" and "in a state of ferocious stupidity." Such descriptions have survived into our own century. According to de Brosses, these early people were at best like terrible children who, without reason or intellect, imagined their playthings to be alive and powerful. De Brosses had missed entirely the nonidolic conception of "power in nature" that is the basis of the religion of most primal peoples, and had mistaken their reverence for nature as a childish sort of animism. But while de Brosses compared primal people to children, he dismissed their capacity for growth. Whereas Western children, according to de Brosses, naturally matured and grew into adulthood, savages must pass their whole lives in an eternal infancy: the impetus of progress being somehow lost to them, and their development never advancing beyond that of a four-year-old civilized child. Thus, de Brosses adumbrated every negative concept of nineteenth-century evolutionists and gave us the legacy that has stifled every effort to convince the dominant society that culture is pluralistic rather than monolithic and that various peoples evolve in their own manner and in their own directions.

De Brosses's conviction of primal stupidity would recur in the subsequent writings of such scholars as Lévy-Brühl, Freud, Frazer, Tylor, and Radin. By de Brosses's time all the most ethnocentric aspects of the Evolutionists were already firmly entrenched as Western social viewpoint. This perspective envisions that all peoples outside the West (including the diminished civilizations of the East) were "living fossils," curiosities forever lost outside the great forward surge of the Western notion of a unilineal progress. De Brosses was convinced that the evolution of the mind had triumphantly culminated in his own enlightened society, which had successfully passed through the intricate obstacle course of nature to achieve (by "overcoming nature") the glorious reality of Western civilization, while contemporary *savages* were seen as hopelessly lost in the maze of nature out of which they could never find their way. In short, the Western societies had transcended nature and outgrown the experiences of primal peoples, leaving them behind and making their *primitive* experience retrograde, useless, and inferior to the focus and priorities of civilized people.

This racist assumption was repeatedly justified by the broadening contention that evolution works in only one positive direction—surging through a predetermined vertical series of stages that all cultures and all peoples must necessarily pass through in order to achieve the status of the West. Thus, the more the behavior of a people resembles the stereotypes of the nineteenth-century image of "cavemen," the further removed they are from civilization and the farther back in the ancestral cave their social and intellectual positions remain forever. Of course, the notion that contemporary people of nonindustrial societies are living fossils is unfounded, yet there are more than a few anthropologists and many popular writers who regularly refer to contemporary primal people, such as the Australian Aborigines, as "remnants of the Stone Age." The popular belief that such primal people's social development must necessarily follow a unilineal evolution is an unprovable assumption. Contrarily, contemporary research indicates that there is little or no reality in the nineteenth-century depiction of early man as described by de Brosses: "barbarous, debilitated, mad, sick, necessitous, and terror-struck." The consensus in the Western world of both primal peoples living today and ancient humanity is self-serving and slanderous.

THE ROMANTIC REVISION

Though the eighteenth century of Turgot and de Brosses is usually called "The Age of Reason," several of its scholars were actually very doubtful about the universality of human reason. One of these skeptics was the pre-Revolutionary French philosopher Jean-Jacques Rousseau (1712–78), who noted dolefully that humanity's many technological advances were not equaled by any noticeable improvements in the social condition of human communities. Thus some thinkers began to wonder if progress were a reality of everyday life or simply a metaphor for the incredible ambition of the West. Some of these distressing social questions were eventually answered negatively by the calamities that attended the French Revolution.

Eventually people began to wonder if perhaps the past might not have been a much better time than the present. Depending upon how this intellectual nostalgia was formulated by the individual, it produced some of the eighteenth century's most outspoken romanticists and some of its most emphatic reactionaries. It also inaugurated a vastly revised view of primal peoples in relation to Western civilization.

Rousseau's conviction that the past may have been more socially significant for the majority of people than the present was uncommon for his time. In his *Discourse on the Origin and Foundation of Inequality among Mankind*, published in 1755, Rousseau envisioned the primary state of humankind as one of great harmony with nature. He depicted early people as living in small contented bands, unencumbered by social constraints or laws, ignorant of the values of gold and silver, and living in accordance with their intuition and emotions in a happy and ideal state that had subsequently been destroyed by civilization. Though Rousseau did not invent or use the term "the Noble Savage" (John Dryden used it first in *The Conquest of Granada*), it was from his romantic vision of the primal past that this highly idealized notion of native peoples sprang. The doctrine of a "return to nature" is incorrectly attributed to Rousseau, who was a realistic thinker fully aware that time could not be reversed. His concept of the "natural man" was purely hypothetical—a metaphor to contrast with the falsities and contradictions of modern civilized lifestyles—and was not intended as a scientific conclusion based on empirical evidence.

Later romanticists, however, were not concerned with what Rousseau originally intended. His positive vision of the past and his dubiousness about the value of reason were well suited to the Romantic Movement's reaction against industry, progress, and contemporary civilization. Romanticism became a pervasive and complicated nineteenth-century movement of thought and art. For the first time since the Renaissance (and its reverent backward look at the classical worlds of Greece and Rome) a glorification of the past became a central theme in the European conception of time. Almost automatically this distrust of progress and reason led to a strong upsurge in the study of primal cultures. The ignoble *savage* became noble—primal people were now depicted as living in a perfect relationship with nature, without strife or greed because they were deemed naturally good and unspoiled by the ravages of civilization.

Like women in the West, primal peoples were thus balanced between two impossible images: innocence or evil, loftiness or lowness, perfection or imperfection. Nowhere in the precepts of eighteenth-century religious rationalism or nineteenth-century romanticism was there room for them to be simply human.

With the demise of Romanticism, the Noble Savage was ordered out of the spotlight of history once again. Whereas the Enlightenment philosophers had earnestly sought universal laws of human evolution in the conviction that what was uniform and natural was also rational, the Romantic thinkers had rejected uniformity entirely and concluded that peoples and their cultures were diversified and that their individuality should be cherished rather than minimized. The post-Romantic inclination of science was to disregard non-Western peoples entirely, since their development appeared to be entirely unrelated to European mentality.

THE INDIAN IN THE WHITE MAN'S HISTORY

The American Indian's destiny was greatly affected by these different ways in which Europeans and Americans conceptualized their observations and intuitions about the origin, nature, and destiny of humankind. It was not through political science but through anthropology and theology that the invaders of the Western Hemisphere sought to understand the totally unexpected peoples they encountered there. Probably no one has provided a more balanced history of the genealogy of the Western view of Native Americans than historian Robert Berkhofer, Jr.

"Since the original inhabitants of the Western Hemisphere neither called themselves by a single term nor understood themselves as a collectivity, the idea and the image of the Indian must be a White conception," Berkhofer has stated. If the word "Indian" and the images and stereotypes that go with it are white inventions, then the first question becomes one that was already old in 1646 when a tribesman asked the Massachusetts missionary John Eliot: "Why do you call us Indians?"

The misnomer, of course, was the result of Columbus's belief that he had found the fabled short route to the East

Indies. What is most curious about the name *Indians* is the fact that even after much debate about the origins and humanity of these aboriginal Americans, and after the geographical realization of the existence of a Western Hemisphere, still use of the word "Indians" persisted. Though the Dominican friar Bartolome de Las Casas heartily defended "Indians" as good and simple people ("Surely these people would be the most blessed in the world if only they worshipped the true God"), and despite the devaluation of the same native people by Juan Gines de Sepulveda ("They not only lack culture but do not even know how to write, and keep no records of their history except certain obscure and vague reminiscences of some things put down in certain pictures"), the name *Indios* persisted as a collective reference to highly diversified and widespread peoples of many different cultures.

It did not take very long for Europeans to understand that the land masses stumbled upon by Columbus were not part of Asia but a whole new world (to Europeans) inhabited by peoples and animals previously unknown, or at least unnamed, in the Scriptures. How was it possible for these unknown peoples to exist? They did not properly fit the story recounted in Genesis of Adam and Eve and the peopling of the earth after the expulsion from the Garden of Eden and the subsequent repopulating of the land by the children of Noah after the destruction of everything by the Flood.

If Indians were outside biblical and classical history, were they really part of the human race? And if they were human, where had they come from and how had they reached this uncharted place now called the Americas?

Orthodox Christians sustained a consistent sense of history, and so they granted that Indians possessed souls and were human beings insofar as scriptural history recounted the creation of humankind in a single godly act—at one time and at one place. Everyone in existence was therefore of one blood and family, possessing the same ancient heritage. This Judeo-Christian monogenetic sense of history required humanity to possess a homogeneity of physique, ethos, and social conscience.

But if Indians were human beings, how could they be traced back to Adam and Eve? The contrasts of lifestyles, languages, colors, and other differences were overwhelming to Europeans. But through comparisons of a few cultural similarities to Europe, Asia, and Africa in word usage, religious ceremonies, and other cultural traits, researchers were able to link Indians with the ancient Greeks, Scythians, and also the fabled biblical Hebrews who provided the essential backdrop of all Western religions, or even the peoples of Atlantis.

Of these many imaginative choices the most popular was the possibility of uncovering a link between American Indians and the Ten Lost Tribes of Israel. As much as this idea has been favored by many professional and lay commentators on Indian origins, the eventual view of the origin of Native Americans was originally formulated as early as 1590 when José de Acosta wrote his *Natural and Moral History of the Indies*, which attempted to solve the riddle of how Indians had managed to travel from the so-called Old World to the New World by suggesting that they had come by way of a land bridge, probably from Asia. This notion of migrations across a temporary land bridge between Asia and Alaska (which is unacceptable to traditional Indians) resolved the question about how Indians reached the Americas, but it left unexplained the elaborate questions concerning how, once in the Western Hemisphere, these "Indians" had produced cultures so widely different from those of other peoples.

Before the twentieth century the most prevalent line of thinking to explain racial differences was based on a conception of degeneration that was born out of the monogenesis of Christian orthodoxy. This viewpoint imagined the continuing degeneration of humankind after the expulsion from Eden to the present time. It was conjectured that idolatry and heathenism, as well as the wide differences in languages and manners, represented the decay of people's grasp of the original knowledge of God at the time of Eden. The long separation of humanity from Eden had led to decay instead of progress, to corruption instead of achievement. Accordingly, Indians were seen as corrupt copies of the Jewish past or were related to degenerated shadows of other past civilizations.

Centuries before the doctrine of evolutionism was formalized, the premise by which Indians were conceptualized had long been formulated. In almost every detail, this metascience has survived as the dominant society's explanation and justification for its exploitation, subjugation, and genocide of primal peoples.

The Christian world view and the cosmogony that lay at its base formed the limits of most white thinking long beyond the 1680s, the decade conventionally said to begin the Age of Reason or the Enlightenment, but after that time thinkers critical of traditional religious and political beliefs gave a new twist to old thoughts sufficient to justify many later scholars in claiming that the modern social sciences began then. For the overwhelming majority of whites who remained orthodox Christians, however, these new thoughts and those of succeeding centuries had to be grafted onto or reconciled with the traditional scriptural history or be rejected. Degeneration therefore remained a powerful analytical tool in white discussions of the Indian well into the nineteenth-century for the orthodox, scholar, and non-scholar alike, even for those persons called the founders of modern American ethnography. Moreover, the basic idea of degeneracy became fused with later interpretations of the Indian through the doctrines of environmentalism, progress, evolutionism, and racism to explain the decline of Native Americans from alcohol, disease, and general deterioration in the face of white contact. In that sense, the idea of Indian degeneracy and decay extended far beyond its religious origins of the Renaissance period to become entwined in and with the very foundations of modern social scientific thinking. In fact the whole Christian interpretation of human diversity in general and Indian origins and differences in particular influenced the fundamental assumptions of the scientific image of the Indian for centuries to come. So long as secular or scientific explanations of human social and cultural variations postulate a single origin for all peoples, then the Christian assumption of a monogenetic origin may be said to have continued its influence. Insofar as white scholars presume the fundamental unity of all humans in psyche and intelligence, then the Christian belief in the brotherhood of all God's souls left its impression on the subsequent social sciences. In these basic outlooks the Christian parenthood of the social scientific image of the Indian becomes apparent.

—ROBERT F. BERKHOFER, JR.

SCIENCE AS HISTORY

By the end of the nineteenth century the realism of Judeo-Christian teleology was rapidly running out and was leaving the Western world with a condition presumed to be ideal by Claude-Henri de Saint-Simon: science had replaced religion and all scientific conviction was now sacred and absolute. The culmination of this Positivist ethos, at least in regard to the human condition, was what anthropologist Marvin Harris (1977) has very aptly called the "biologization of history." Science had elaborated upon the logical extremes of race in order to produce an "objective" racism. Copious field work along Positivist lines was undertaken: including analyses of religion, primarily, as well as governments, marriage, family, education, general division of labor, techniques of hunting and fishing, language, and customs of burial, birth, and initiation.

A comparative method arose by which the enormous

body of data of one culture was contrasted with another. The results of these efforts generally confirmed the assumptions that had prompted racial attitudes in the first place. Researchers were convinced that the fundamental mentality of the earliest *Homo sapiens* closely resembled that of contemporary "primitive" peoples, while the behavior and concepts of modern Americans and Europeans were drastically different from those of prehistoric humanity and the "primitives" of modern times. Entailed in these comparisons from the outset and seemingly proven by the findings was the premise that the present conditions of primal peoples could be taken to represent the early stages of present civilized societies. As we have already noted, primal peoples were regarded by science as "living fossils."

In 1767 Edinburgh University professor Adam Ferguson wrote: "It is in their [the Indians'] present condition that we are to behold, as in a mirror, the features of our own progenitors." In the theoretical language of the eighteenth century, this attitude was leading to a "science" of race that built an analogy between the life process of a single human being and the history of the entire species. In France and Scotland, in particular, a philosophical history was produced that formulated a series of stages of societal evolution that all races had to pass through in order to ascend to the heights of progress exemplified by Europe at the time. Essentially this concept envisioned a parallel between a person's development from infancy, youth, and adulthood and all humankind's passage from savagery, barbarism, and civilization.

This perspective had and still has an enormous appeal to those still orthodox in their basic, if nonreligious, Christian worldview. As Berkhofer points out: "Only under assumptions of a common and constant human nature, the uniform workings of immutable laws in human affairs, and the abstraction of the natural from the accidental in history could thinkers of the time compare customs among widely divergent lifestyles, range them into a series of gradations, and present them as the history of *all* human development and achievement. Out of this intellectual context in the eighteenth century came the new word *civilization* with its modern meaning."

This survey of the science of race in the eighteenth century helps to clarify aspects of the racial attitudes dominating the late nineteenth century. The aim of so-called raciology—the "scientific study of racial differences"—was transformed into a search for some substantial data that would confirm popular racial inferences based on prejudice and casual, biased observation. The comparative methods of the eighteenth-century thinkers offended nineteenth-century scholars far more than did the racist conclusions drawn by their comparisons. The new approach to this dilemma was an attempt to place the subject of race upon a more scientific basis through the detailed and quantified study of anatomy.

One of the most curious aspects of this kind of justification of racism was the invention of the cephalic index (length-breadth ratio), which purported to study the size of the brain and the shape of the skull under the general heading of craniometry or craniology. This dubious science was of particular interest in the United States insofar as it served the pro-slavery debate by pointing out "the inherent inferiority of blacks." From the measurement of hundreds of skulls, a Philadelphian physician named Samuel George Morton (1799–1851) and his disciples of the so-called American School concluded that the skulls of various races ranged in size from a mean of 92 cubic inches for the contemporary Caucasian races to 79 cubic inches for the American Indian races and 75 cubic inches for the Hottentots and Australian Bushmen. These measurements were seen to prove conclusively the superiority of whites over all other races. Craniometry was freely used to justify the U.S. policies toward Indians and blacks. Social evolution was fused with an idea about mental capacity, and mental capacity was assumed to be a function of cranial size. Morton concluded, therefore, that "lower races not only possessed darker skins and bad manners but their organic equipment was also inferior." As anthropologist Marvin Harris has pointed out, it was assumed that, according to scientific racism, the reason white-skinned peoples ruled the world and epitomized civilization was not accidental, but an inevitable result of biological inheritance. In short, nonwhites were pervasively and irreversibly inferior.

What eighteenth-century scholars tended to ascribe to the progress of reason or social conditions in the history of nations, late nineteenth- and early twentieth-century social scientists attributed to the mental superiority in the history of some races. Evolution and raciology influenced the newly developing field of psychology, and in turn that new discipline's findings were taken to support racial differences. The most important phase of this history was the study of instinct as the mental feature common to animals and humans. Since "savages" were presumed to be closest to the animal stage, they were also presumed, therefore, to be creatures of instinct. Only advanced races could apply their ratiocinative powers to their situation and thereby produce literature, religions, and constitutional governments. Thus, once again, science confirmed the longtime stereotyped characterization of primal peoples.

This form of scientific racism prevailed well into the early decades of the twentieth century as part of the social sciences of the United States. By the 1930s, however, a variety of new impulses were beginning to countermand racist attitudes by asserting new ideas of cultural pluralism that provided a context for the conceptualization of culture and cultural relativity. By the mid-twentieth century racism had been fully discredited by science and remained essentially a political weapon used by those who endeavored to subjugate peoples for economic and political motives. It should be remembered, however, that the enlightened anthropology ushered in by the German-trained American scientist Franz Boas was as much a reflection of his times as the conceptions of earlier scholars mirrored their own worldviews.

In this way we are able to determine that when Western science progresses, it often opens vaster mysteries to its scrutiny. As Loren Eiseley has pointed out, "Science frequently discovers that it must abandon or modify what it once believed. Sometimes it ends by accepting what it has previously scorned. The simplistic idea that science marches undeviatingly down an ever broadening highway can scarcely be sustained by the historian of ideas."

Science, and the philosophy based upon it, is one of the numerous ways by which we ritualize our experience. That ritual is undergoing constant alteration.

THE DECLINE OF WESTERN CERTITUDE

Scholars are following closely upon the words of philosopher Alfred North Whitehead, who said: "It is the business of the future to be dangerous . . . the major advances in civilization are processes that all but wreck the societies in which they occur." For instance, sociobiologist Daniel G. Freedman ponders inherent racial and ethnic differences in babies and reports in his 1979 book *Human Sociobiology* that "striking differences in temperament and behavior among ethnic groups show up in babies only a few days old."

"Given these data," Freedman asserts at the close of his argument, "I think it is a reasonable conclusion that we should drop two long-cherished myths: (1) No matter what our ethnic background, we are all born alike; (2) culture and biology are separate entities. Clearly, we are biosocial creatures in everything we do and say, and it is time that anthropologists, psychologists, and population geneticists start speaking the same language. In light of what we know, only a truly holistic, multidisciplinary approach makes sense."

At the same time, Marvin Harris (1974) has fundamentally redesigned the way we are supposed to look at the much maligned "caveman" who was so animatedly berated by nineteenth-century scholars. "The Victorians exaggerated the material poverty of the so-called savages and at the same time inflated the benefits of industrial 'civilization.' They pictured the Old Stone Age as a time of great fear and insecurity, when people spent their days ceaselessly searching for food and their nights huddled about fires in comfortless caves besieged by saber-toothed tigers. It isn't easy to overcome this kind of indoctrination." Harris goes on to point out that Stone Age populations lived healthier lives than did many people who came after them. Moreover, Stone Age hunters worked fewer hours for their sustenance than do typical Chinese peasants—"or, despite their unions, modern-day factory workers." They knew how to make artificial shelters, for contrary to popular belief, "cavemen" did not live in caves but appear to have used their caves and rock overhangs for ceremonial purposes.

Archaeologists in Russia and Czechoslovakia have found traces of elaborate animal-skin dwellings set in shallow pits 40 feet long by 12 feet wide, dating from more than 20,000 years ago. That is where so-called cavemen lived. The skeletal remains of the early hunters themselves indicate that they were usually well nourished. As for the inherent stupidity and blind instinctuality of early humankind, the anatomical structure as well as the stupendous expressiveness of the paintings of animals on the walls of caves in France and Spain provide a picture of a people not unlike ourselves, a people possessing an exceptional intelligence in their observations of nature and their grasp of its spiritual impact. There is today a conclusive opinion among most scholars that the mentality and emotional makeup of *Homo sapiens* of the Stone Age were remarkably similar to the fundamental character, intelligence, and imagination of contemporary humans. The great chasm that Western civilization has built between itself and "primitive" people is part of the complex mythology of the West, confirming its racist assumption of its superiority and its divine right to prevail no matter the loss in the customs, property, rights, and survival of others.

If one adds to these Western myths about nonwhites the conceptions of progress and evolution, Robert Berkhofer, Jr. concludes:

> then one arrives at the fundamental premises behind much of white understanding of the Indian from about the middle of the eighteenth century to very recent times. Under these conceptions civilization was destined to triumph over savagery, and so the Indian was to disappear either through death or through assimilation into the larger, more progressive white society. For white Americans during this long period of time, the only good Indian was indeed a dead Indian—whether through warfare or through assimilation. . . . In the twentieth century anthropologists rushed to salvage ethnography from the last living members left over from the ethnographic present, and historians treated Indians as "dead" after early contact with whites. In these ways modern Native Americans and their contemporary lifestyles have largely disappeared from the white imagination—unless modern Indian activism reverses this historic trend for longer than the recurring but transitory white enthusiasm for things Indian.

The overview of the dominant society's image and idea of American Indians and other primal peoples vacillates between the precepts of Western religion and the concepts of Western science. With the emergence of a relativistic viewpoint in science, with the constant onslaught of observations and hypotheses that countermand the rituals of Judeo-Chris-

tian dogma, and with today's deeply felt and daringly facilitated humanism, the first shock waves of a "cultural earthquake" are awakening Western humankind to the dizzying
realization that it is not alone . . . that there are other
worlds.* These "lessons of the earthquake" have aroused in
us the possibilities of Western transience and fallibility. The
West has grown positively sick of looking at itself, and it is
trying to catch a dim glimpse of some vague "otherness,"
some potential alternative, some different reality previously
hidden beyond the self-congratulatory mirrors of a stifled
and windowless civilization.

LESSONS OF THE EARTHQUAKE

> We in the western world have rushed eagerly to embrace the
> future—and in so doing we have provided that future with a
> strength it has derived from us and our endeavors. Now,
> stunned, puzzled and dismayed, we try to withdraw from the
> embrace, not of a necessary tomorrow, but of that future
> which we have invited and of which, at last, we have grown
> perceptibly afraid.
>
> —LOREN EISELEY

For Aristotle any point of view other than realism did not
even arise; the common-sense observation of events and objects exists independent of our interpretations of them. This
naive realism, or "practical fiction" as the Existentialists have
called it, was the dominant frame of reference of Western
history for hundreds of years. It culminated in nineteenth-
century science that thrived on the Cartesian concept of consciousness and upon the raciology and concept of progress
that we have already explored. Twentieth-century science,

---

* A nontechnical account of the "new physics" and its philosophical ramifi-
cations can be found in *The Dancing Wu Li Masters: An Overview of the New Physics* by Gary Zukav, published too late to be assimilated into this text. Zukav develops a point of view scientifically parallel to the aesthetic ideas discussed in
this book.

however, has fundamentally altered its own sense of what is constituted by the word "realism." The strict laws of Empiricism and Positivism have not so much been discarded as ignored in the pursuit of a worldview that requires subtle and flexible truths.

The researches of Freud, Jung, Darwin, Frazer, Einstein, and many other pioneers of a new mentality largely rejected the neat patterns of nature as conceived by Descartes. Such highly diverse philosophers as Henri Bergson (1859) and Martin Heidegger (1889) became determined for the first time in the history of the West to take the great leap beyond reason in order to see how reason itself might look from the outside—that is, from the point of view of some other potential of comprehension granted the human animal. What such philosophers were proposing in the early 1900s was a new interpretation of reason and its various operations. For the next seventy-five years the fundamental way we think about the world was drastically altered by the radical and persuasive doctrines of Phenomenology and Existentialism particularly. Then, starting about 1940, science also broke out of the Aristotelian cosmos. Thus philosophy had changed the way we think about the world and science was changing the way we see the world. All that remained of Aristotelian realism was Faustian Man himself, seeing and thinking about the world in new ways but continuing *to experience* the world very much as he had done since about 300 B.C.

This crucial fragmentation of Faustian Man has provided the gaping holes in the Great Wall and all the other intellectual barriers that for centuries successfully held back "the terrible floodtide of barbarians."

"History and anthropology teach us that a human society cannot long survive unless its members are psychologically contained within a central living myth. Such a myth provides the individual his reason for being. To the ultimate questions of human existence it provides answers which satisfy the most developed and discriminating members of the society. And if the creative, intellectual minority is in harmony with the prevailing myth, the other layers of society will follow its lead and may even be spared a direct encounter with the fateful question of the meaning of life," Jungian philosopher Edward F. Edinger has written. He continues by saying that it is evident to thoughtful people that Western society no longer has a viable, functioning myth. It therefore has no basis to affirm life.

This reference to Western society does not imply simply the West as it is designated geographically, as it appears on maps. Edmund Husserl has written:

> In the spiritual sense, it is clear that to Europe belong the English dominions, the United States, etc., but not, however, the Eskimos or Indians, or the Gypsies. Clearly the title Europe designates the unity of a spiritual life and a creative activity—with all its aims, interests, cares, and troubles, with its plans, its establishments, its institutions. I mean we [Europeans] feel that in our European humanity there is an innate entelechy that thoroughly controls the changes in the European image and gives to it the sense of a development in the direction of an ideal image of life and of being, as moving toward an eternal pole.

Therefore the Western world is a concept and not a geographical place, and its *ideal image* has lost that myth of "an eternal pole" that once guided it.

In the last decades of the twentieth century we are finding ourselves with visions of black holes and of a negative universe that is adjoined to ours but opposite from our own cosmos. We are asked to grasp the conception of event horizons and clones and other precepts that, though nonrational, are nonetheless clearly not irrational. We find ourselves quite literally in that impossible position on the outside of reason where we are for the first time finding out how to use that other power of comprehension and vision granted the human animal. In this way, we are beginning in the West to experience the world that the new science invented during our century, and we are discarding, like the outgrown skin of a reptile, the Faustian mentality that was supposed to be the real and final image of Western humanity.*

It seems to me that this new, emerging mentality is strikingly similar to the sensibility of those who see the world through primal minds. And thus "progress" has ironically verified the validity of peoples the West has been persistently trying to eradicate as obsolete, primitive, and useless.

Nowhere is this new sensibility more apparent in the West than in the contemporary arts. As the French philosopher Maurice Merleau-Ponty (1908–61) has stated: these special uses of the imagination by artists "give visible existence to what profane vision believes to be invisible . . . in fact they exist only at the threshold of profane vision; and so they are not seen by everyone." (1964c).

ART AS A WITNESS TO THE EARTHQUAKE

> One earthquake does more to demonstrate our vulnerability and mortality than the whole history of philosophy.
> —MAURICE MERLEAU-PONTY (1964c)

The enormous upheaval that has overtaken Western mentality of the twentieth century reverberates in all the arts. Nowhere is this "earthquake of ideas" more visible and experiential than in art, among the works of painters, poets, authors, choreographers, and composers—people who apparently deal with fictions rather than Positivist facts. And

---

* A major formulation, for instance, of the New Physics (the Copenhagen Interpretation of Quantum Mechanics, as it is known) is the theory called the Many Worlds Interpretation, which envisions an endlessly proliferating number of different branches of reality. According to this theory, whenever a choice is made in the universe between one possible event and another, the universe splits into different branches.

yet the Western scholar has finally come to see such fictions as variations upon factuality. As D. P. Gallagher wrote when speaking of modern Latin American literature, "Latin American novelists very often seek to create a reality that is quite deliberately *alternative* to the one they are living in. The lesson is not missed that although the new creation may well be fictive, the society it is aiming to replace is fictive too." This, of course, is one of the lessons of the earthquake.

In contemporary art we discover not only the decline of the West but also the efforts of artists to discover personal myths in which their works might live. At the moment, when the content of the work of art has lost its traditional ideological function in society, the forms of the art have become the new ideologies. The question of ideology was not relevant when various Western societies had one overriding set of assumptions: a stabilizing value system that pervaded the entire community. An ancient Greek or Christian artist had no conscience to square: he worked in a unified process of thought and production. The change came about when the meaning behind the word "art" ceased to be the carrier of an ideology and became known as its own ideology.

Spectators are able to enter a Renaissance painting. They can walk mentally into it and move about because the painting provides the illusion of being a mirror image of the expected reality. When the modern artist of the twentieth century overthrew the Renaissance concept of space and illusion, a barrier was put up that prevented us from "realistically" entering into the world of the painting. The artist expelled us from the work of art and returned us to the position of primal people who have usually regarded art conceptually—not as an object of the eye but as an experience of the mind, as a ritual form.

The victors of the Western world have won everything—and in the process have lost themselves. Those people who work in art rather than in industry feel this loss very deeply.

They are attempting to create rites of their own to compensate for the lack of rituals integral to their societies. Most of the great artists of our century have built a mysterious self through their art to fill the vacuum left by the lack of public ceremonial life. And what, after all, is this marvelous, ritual self? It is an appearance, an apparition if you like. It springs from what we do but it is not what we are. It is something else. In watching a ritual you do not see what is physically before you. What you see is an interaction of forces by which something else arises. Those who see only what is before them are blind to all the other potentials of experience. Ritual, like art, requires us to *really* see. What we see is a virtual image that is not unreal, for when we are confronted by it, it really does exist. The image in a mirror is such an image; so is a rainbow. It seems to stand on earth or in the clouds, but it really "stands" nowhere. It is only visible, not tangible. It is the unspeakable, the ineffable made visible, made experiential.

Contemporary artists are fascinated by technology, but they like to play with it rather than use it industriously. They use technology to produce apparitions, and this is heresy in terms of the Faustian dream. Artists are using the new technology to destroy technology, to reverse the process of specificity and specialization. They are using technology to produce that ambiguity at the core of ritual. Naturally this counterproductive urge of artists and phenomenologists is nonsensical and repulsive to those striving for the stars. They want artists to be technical virtuosi. They want *real* art. They want lots of fantastic technique and tasty illusions. They want to be uplifted—by rockets and supersonic aircraft. Somewhere over the rainbow, no doubt. But what they need, and what the Western mind needs, is more rainbows.

"The Western artist's preoccupation," art historian Hans Hess has written, "is with the state of art, the meaning of art."

The artist's individual struggle to save himself and his art are the unconscious responses to the threat in social reality. By stating the problem in this manner, that man is reacting within and against a social framework, one does not detract from the struggles and victories of the artist. In the process of changing the pictorial form, a whole aesthetic arose which had its roots in the ideas of society. How the rediscovery of the [primal] and the naive was transmuted by the painters to account for the new choice of subject-matter and the complete disappearance of the object is the whole development of modern art. There appear in the imagination of the West what can only be called monsters, if seen under the aesthetic of the past; masks and [primal] images make their appearance for the first time in European painting. Already in the nineteenth-century the process of reappraisal of the past had begun. The European aesthetic was changing from the classical ideal. From mid-century onwards a reappraisal of simplicity and strength of [primal] vision and hieratic earnestness develops in opposition to the art of the Salon. Gauguin opposed refined art to [primal] art, and stated: "[Primal] art stems from the spirit . . . so-called fine art from sense impressions." In this search for new expressive forms, the modern artist travelled over the whole range of the world of art and reflected the upheaval of the decline of the West. It was the modern artist who looked back, not the Stone Age which looked forward.

The bankruptcy of public truth in the West opened the way to outside influences that had been previously ignored. Among these numerous influences was the impact of primal art, which directly and indirectly made a profound and lasting change not only in the way Western artists depict reality but also in the way the general public thinks about reality.

Just as twentieth-century philosophers have sought an alternative rational facility in the hope of comprehending reason and its operation from the outside (rather than from the internalized Aristotelian vantage), so creative artists have employed elements of primal and Asian art in an effort to revaluate and comprehend Western art traditions from a position outside and beyond Aristotelian realism. In a very real sense, then, contemporary artists have discovered the avant-garde in the caves of Altamira.

I should make it clear that in discussing the influences of primal and Asian arts on the West I do not intend to call attention to the superficial kinds of atmospheric ethos which have long passed for exotic impact on Western art: such as Puccini's evocation of Japan in *Madama Butterfly*, Fokine's balletic cartoon of Arabia called *Scheherazade*, or Karl May's Germanic notions of Native Americans found in his fictive Winatu novels. Such *fake-lore*, as it has aptly been called, is an entirely different matter from the genuine interest in primal folklore that was the concern of Europeans and Americans during the first half of this century.

NEW ART FROM OLD WAYS

Although many different ideologies have influenced modern art, it is impossible to discuss the foundations of twentieth-century aesthetics without giving special attention to the way in which primal art became a visible force in the changes taking place in the arts of Europe and America. As Edward Lucie-Smith points out in *Art Now*, "Gauguin was prepared to go farther than the Romanticists. He looked among a [primal] people, still with the vestiges of their pre-Christian tribal culture, for the qualities that he thought were missing from contemporary European society. And in this sense he was one of the founders of the cult of barbarism which swept through advanced circles on the eve of the First World War. Henri Matisse shared the feeling with many of his contemporaries that the society they lived in was stiflingly elaborate as well as stiflingly conventional."

Maurice de Vlaminck and André Derain altered the entire development of Western art when they discovered African masks and conveyed their admiration for these wondrously carved artifacts to the young Picasso and Matisse. Art historians frequently point out that the most significant element about Picasso's revolutionary painting *Les Demoiselles d'Avignon* is the fact it ushered in the artist's so-called Negro Period, which led, in turn, to the birth of Cubism. African artists tend to use faceted forms, in which the planes of carvings are distinguished from one another by a firm and visible channel or boundary. This faceted surface suggests the multiple viewpoints of European Analytical Cubism.

When the British sculptor Henry Moore visited Paris in 1925, he spent some time at the Trocadero Museum where he saw a plaster cast of the reclining figure of Chac Mool—a rain power-figure of the Toltec and Maya cultures whose center was at Chichen Itza in Yucatán, Mexico, in about the ninth century A.D. This unique figure, carved out of limestone, reclines with its head turned at a perfect right angle to the body and with its knees drawn up. There are numerous such carved figures with breastplates in the form of a stylized butterfly. The figure is usually shown wearing bracelets, ankle rings, and sandals. The hands hold a flat receptacle on the stomach believed to have held sacrifices.

Moore became obsessed by this sculpture to such an extent that his entire career was fundamentally influenced by its form. In an article on "Primitive Art" in *The Listener* (1941), Moore wrote that "Mexican sculpture, as soon as I found it, seemed to me true and right, perhaps because I at once hit on similarities in it with some eleventh-century carvings I had seen as a boy on Yorkshire churches. Its 'stoniness,' by which I mean its truth to material, its tremendous power without loss of sensitiveness, its astonishing variety and fertility of form-invention and its approach to a full three-dimensional conception of form, make it unsurpassed in my opinion by any other period of stone sculpture."

Herbert Read has pointed out in his book on Henry Moore that what the sculptor incarnates in his famous reclining figures is, first of all, a metaphorical comparison of the human (especially female) body and the earth eroded by natural forces into hills and hollows; and, beyond this, an aesthetic delight in the sensuous forms of the human body itself.

These numerous examples of artists who were fundamentally influenced by primal art in the twentieth century is not simply a way of praising primal mentality by proxy—but is intended to point out the curious fact that after some twelve-to-seventeen thousand years during which Europeans were aesthetically unaware of the existence of primal arts, suddenly their influence became the most powerful catalyst of Western twentieth-century modernism.

Authors such as Bernard Rudofsky and Vincent Scully have made valuable observations about the relationships of primal architecture and the focuses of modern Western building. Literary analyst Leslie Fiedler has demonstrated the primal sensibility implicit in the mythos of the American West. As Fiedler has pointed out, America was regarded as a "new world" by Europeans—a world with a North, South, and East, along with a mysterious West that was *closed.* By whom? Perhaps by God, who had placed the earthly paradise of Eden in the West and closed it off from man until the present days of a glorious new birth for humankind in this vast "New World." As Fiedler has shown, a very profound influence came out of this vision of the American West that has basically affected the entire literature of the Western Hemisphere, from the "Magic Realism" of contemporary Latin American authors to Americanists, folklorists, and fake-lorists such as Mark Twain, James Fenimore Cooper, Ernest Hemingway, and Ken Kesey.

Western music was also greatly changed by encounters with the music of primal peoples. Debussy was very interested in Javanese gamelan music. Debussy prophesied "a starker, barer kind of music" that he found emerging in the music of a young composer named Igor Stravinsky, whose *Le sacre du printemps* the elderly Debussy heard in a performance on two pianos.

The music of Béla Bartók was, of course, deeply swayed by elements of Hungarian folk music, which he collected and studied. As Bartók's biographer Serge Moreux has stated: "Explicitly or implicitly, folk-music underlies all his work." Moreux quotes Bartók himself: "This whole study of folk-music was of capital importance in enabling me to free myself from the tyranny, which I had up to then accepted, of the major and minor modal systems."

Though Igor Stravinsky, during the composing of *Le sacre du printemps* (a ballet score for Serge Diaghilev), was not preoccupied with folkloric scholarship and worked instead out of the imagination, his aims were not unlike Bartók's at least in terms of his reverence for his primal subject matter. "I wanted to compose the libretto with N. K. Roerich," Stravinsky wrote N. F. Findeizen in 1912, "because who else could help, who else knows the secret of our ancestors' close feeling for the earth? . . ."

The list of Western contemporary artists and philosophers influenced by primal mentality is very long and elaborate. Jacob Epstein, Modigliani, Brancusi, Dubuffet, and Giacometti are surely prominent among them. So too was the great Spanish poet Federico García Lorca, whose imagery flowed from the Andalusia of gypsies and Moors. The Russian nationalist composers evoked elements of pre-Christian rituals. And in the music of Edgar Varèse, Harry Partch, George Crumb, Lucia Dlugoszewski, Lou Harrison, Alan Hovhaness, and the Minimalist composers such as Terry Riley, Steve Reich, and Philip Glass there is the unmistakable and often highly significant imprint of primal mentality.

Martha Graham once told photographer Barbara Morgan

that if she had not attended the ritual dances of Pueblo Indians in New Mexico during the late 1920s she would never have created her revolutionary work entitled *Primitive Mysteries*—which changed all future efforts in the then-new "modern interpretative dance."

Choreographers such as José Limon, Erick Hawkins, and Lester Horton consciously reflected numerous elements of ceremonial dance in their highly innovative and individual works for the stage. They collectively gave rise to a whole new way of thinking about theatrical dancing.

In some curious way the mentality, vision, and even the formal techniques of primal peoples provided a whole generation of Western artists and thinkers with new ways of seeing, feeling, and depicting their world. The slow collapse of many Western ideologies has made way for this uncommon influence from primal cultures. This cultural exchange was clearly a unique occurrence in world history; the most conspicuous example of the unlimited impact made upon a "superior" culture by primal peoples. And yet there is something about this transaction that recalls many prior empires that collapsed and were overrun by so-called barbarians—barbarians who revitalized or replaced failed worlds. It seems that these outsiders have often been the precious reservoir of humanity's most fertile energies and insights—a constant spring from which towering cultures arise—Greeks out of Minoans, Romans out of Greeks, Toltecs out of Maya, Franks out of Romans, the Empire of the West out of the Frankish domain, Europe out of the Empire of the West, and the United States of America out of Europe.

AFTER THE EARTHQUAKE

Picasso evolved a language that has altered the course of art—and even of life—in our century. Even after Picasso began to live in Paris, his work stayed fairly conservative by contemporary standards. Only with his discovery of Iberian and African sculpture did his work begin to change radically, and then the changes were swift and irreversible . . . it culminates in the shattering dislocations and [primal] "African" faces of some of the figures in *Les Demoiselles d'Avignon*, for me the greatest painting of this century.

—JOHN ASHBERY

Today the West understands the cosmos in ways that were previously incomprehensible. We are open to kinds of experience once entirely remote from us. We grasp both time and space in a drastically new way both because of the accelerations of our technology and also because our artists have made startling and alien visions a commonplace in our films, paintings, music, dances, and literature. Philosophers like Carl Jung have given us a grasp of archetypes that transcend stereotypes, of the reality existing within our dreams—elements of an unlimited consciousness once quite beyond our comprehension. In countless ways the West has found itself in closer and closer communion with a mentality it once considered little more than the pathetic confusions of some dark and remote ancestral childhood. In this rather curious fashion the sentinels who guard the bridges against fearsome barbarians have opened the way and made it possible—perhaps for the first time in our planet's history—for people to transcend their cultural isolation. The way between us is open, and now in a conscious and significant manner we might look across at one another and make some profound sense out of our differences. Think of the remarkable exchanges we might have! Given enough time and patience, we might even come to believe in one another.

II

ASPECTS OF
THE PRIMAL
MIND

3

IMAGE

The reality in which [primal] peoples move is itself mystical.
—LUCIEN LÉVY-BRÜHL

IMAGE-MAKING

The arts are conceptually discrete—composers do not write "tunes" and artists do not make "pictures," let alone paint houses—they are involved in an infinitely more complex, idealized, and conceptualized act.

It was not always that way. At one time, and as recently as the Renaissance, the major difference between, for example, a folk song and a madrigal was one of refinement rather than concept. The "conceptualizing" of art into something special called "Art" produced a wide separation between commonplace experience and *specialized* forms of expression. For primal peoples, on the other hand, the relationship between experience and expression has remained so direct and spontaneous that they usually do not possess a word for art. They do, however, possess a concept of *living*, which, in Western interpretation, might seem like art.

Among a primal people there is an exquisite homogeneity and a wholeness that puts each tribal member in direct touch with his or her culture and with its carefully prescribed and perpetuated forms. Just as each member of the tribe is—by Western standards—intrinsically merged with every other member, so too is the individual immersed in the vast range of tribal experiences that the West calls "culture." The idiosyncratic characteristics that gradually arose in Europe during the Renaissance and became known as *individuality* and *originality* are virtually unknown among Indians and other aboriginal craftsmen, whose work is considered no more rarefied or conceptually discrete than that of the farmer, shaman, hunter, or any other person of the tribe. Art is unnamed because it is part of a continuum wider and more inclusive than the Western idea of reality. Paul Radin, one of the foremost students of American Indian religion, makes a strong point of this alternative vision of reality. The Indian does not make the separation into personal as contrasted with impersonal in the Western sense at all. What he seems to be interested in is the whole question of existence and reality; and everything that is perceived by the senses, thought of, felt, and dreamed of, truly exists for him . . . as *inseparable* aspects of the real.

An *image* is a visual counterpart of that reality. There are many different ways of making and experiencing images. And no process more plainly depicts that immensity of differences between peoples than their unique grasp of image-making. There are, in fact, instances in which the fundamental mentality of peoples is so dissimilar that they cannot understand the means (let alone the messages) by which experience becomes transformed into expression in an alien culture. Such a meeting of irreconcilable minds took place in the northern Plains of America during the nineteenth century.

The twenty-sixth day of February, 1852, was filled with wind and snow at Fort Union, near the mouth of the Yellowstone River. The Swiss artist and explorer Rudolph Friederich Kurz had come a long way from his homeland to observe and to draw the "wild" Indians of America. What he found in the Northwest was a people of exceptionally refined artistic skills. "They drew very well indeed for savages," he wrote in his *Journal* (written 1846–52 but not published until 1937 by the Smithsonian Institution). "We must take into consideration," he conceded, "that the human form is not represented in the same manner by all nations; on the contrary, each nation has its own conventional manner."

Kurz's appreciation of such cultural difference was exceptional for his day. But for all his admirable insights into other cultures, he found it exceedingly difficult to apply his uncommon liberality. One encounter with a Sioux Indian "artist" dramatizes the dissimilarities in the way various peoples produce images and it also tells us a great deal about the primal mind in relation to the Western mind.

"While I was sketching one afternoon," wrote Kurz, "a Sioux visited me. To my surprise he brought along two interesting drawings of his own. While I worked he glanced over my shoulder and nodded rather sympathetically. It turned out that he was not at all satisfied with my drawings. He explained to me that he could do better."

With considerable amusement, Kurz provided drawing paper and ink. The Indian began at once to make drawings. After producing a number of very handsome figures, the Sioux drew a man on horseback. Though the animal was depicted from the side, the Indian artist had drawn both of the man's legs on the side of the horse which was in view.

"No . . . no," Kurz exclaimed, hoping to correct the error at once. "You must draw only one leg because, you see, the body of the horse conceals the other leg."

Again the Sioux nodded sympathetically at the befuddled Kurz. To strengthen his argument, the Swiss artist quickly sketched a profile view of a man on a horse. The Indian gazed at it and then explained politely that Kurz's representation of a rider with only one leg was "not at all satisfactory."

"But this is the way it *must* be drawn," Kurz insisted. "Only one leg should be visible!"

"Ah," the Sioux said softly, "but, you see, a man has *two* legs."

To the Indian the fact that one limb is concealed by the

horse's body is not the point. The rule that art must imitate appearances is arbitrary and represents just one idea of reality—though it happens to be the pervasive reality of the dominant culture. Indians are interested in something more essential.

IMAGE AND ITS ASPECTS

Art is a way of *seeing*, and what we see in art helps to define what we understand by the word "reality." We do not all see the same things. Though the dominant societies usually presume that their vision represents the sole truth about the world, each society (and often individuals within the same society) sees reality uniquely. The complex process by which the artist transforms the act of seeing into a vision of the world is one of the consummate mysteries of the arts— one of the reasons that art is inseparable from religion and philosophy for most tribal peoples. This act of envisioning and then engendering a work of art represents an important and powerful ritual. Making images is one of the central ways by which humankind ritualizes experience and gains personal and tribal access to the ineffable . . . the unspeakable and ultimate substance of reality.

Art historian Herbert Read (1965) makes an important observation about the primal way of making animal images, which reflects this ritual-making mentality. "In such representations there is no attempt to conform with the exact but casual appearances of animals; and no desire to evolve an ideal type of animal. Rather from an intense awareness of the nature of the animal, its movements and its habits, the artist is able to select just those features which best denote its vitality, and by exaggerating these and distorting them until they cohere in some significant rhythms and shape, he produces a representation which conveys to us the very *essence* of the animal."

Since the time of the Gothic sensibility of the twelfth century, this grasp of essences rather than casual appearances
has ceased to be a dominant vision in Western art. Only during the twentieth century have artists again become interested in the essential interpretation of reality rather than the
imitation of its casual appearances. It is significant that much
of the impulse behind the revelations of modern art derives
from the influences of primal art, at the same time that
much of the Western interest in the alternative mentalities
of primal peoples is made possible and coherent by the aesthetic insights of modern art itself.

"The best tribute to preliterary art," wrote Harry Elmer
Barnes in his classic *An Intellectual and Cultural History of the
Western World* (1941), "is the fact that some of the most advanced schools of painters and sculptors of the present day
are going back to [primal art] for their inspiration. Primitivism in modern art is, consciously or not, a groping towards
the aesthetics of precivilized man, an attempt to catch *the
pure vision* found in his sculptured objects, wall paintings,
and engravings."

But what is this *pure vision* of which Barnes wrote, and
what is this "intense awareness of the *nature* of the animal"
itself that Herbert Read described with such respect? Surely
it is an experience almost entirely outside the focus of Western mentality. The intellectual finesse of scholars has been
capable of naming it, but are people of the West in any way
capable of really *knowing* the process by which this purity of
vision and this intense awareness of things unto themselves
become manifested in an artist and in his work of art?

The startling revision of attitudes toward "precivilized
man" has truly brought alternative worlds into focus; yet
this new interpretation of neglected realms of human experience may make them far more visible than comprehensible. The revised Western vantage point can be just as ethnocentric as the obsolescent assumption that extant

"primitives" are windows upon the Neanderthal world. In other words, we are still presuming that the values of one culture are apt tools with which to measure the values of another culture. The error of this kind of thinking can be seen in the way Western scholars have evaluated the motivation of primal thinking. Sigmund Freud achieved a major new insight when he formalized a conception of the "unconscious mind," but he described it as an unruly and irrational domain and the source of a force so violent and primitive that "civilization" could only be achieved through the systematic suppression of the animal nature of human beings that was asssumed to "live" in this unconscious mind.

It stands to reason that this very negative and atomistic evaluation of the "primitive" aspects of the human mind would result in a misconception of those alien worlds brought into focus by the recent revision of attitudes toward "precivilized man." Vision, dream, inspiration, ritual, and even art—by Freudian appraisal—are mere rumbles of a subterranean psychic volcano that must be kept capped lest it destroy civilization. Matters of kinship and dominancy are based upon a Freudian battle of the sexes as well as the everlasting stresses of something called "penis envy"—which would seem to have far more significance to central European (Judaic) patriarchal mentality than it does to the social realities of most primal peoples. Art, myth, and even the essential perspective of "precivilized man" are seen by Freudian stereotypes as symptoms of an epidemical human disease—the rampant, consuming, and primitive pox of instincts from out of our animal legacy.

It is very fortunate that the highly linear perspective of Freud has been reenvisioned by a number of scholars, including his famous disciple, Carl Jung, who recast them in far less biblical terms, which do not indulge in Judeo-Christian values and which therefore provide an evaluation of human mentality capable of describing the *many* worlds of *Homo sapiens.*

There is a Jungian implication in Read's description of so-called Animal Style in primal art. He commented, you recall, that the representation of animal forms does not attempt to deal with exact appearances. "Rather," he suggests, "from an intense awareness of the *nature* of the animal" the artist is able to select just those qualities that best cohere to the very *essence* of the animal's being. What Read seems to be saying is that this remarkable primal awareness is achieved through something other than observation—which is, of course, the usual approach to reality in the West. By contrast, this unorthodox kind of primal awareness is achieved through *trans-/formation*—and that is clearly not a Western conception.

THE BODY AS AN ORGAN OF PERCEPTION

It will not be easy to explain what I mean by *transformation*. The term smacks more than a little of science fiction, and it describes the kind of peculiar experience that is not a conscious capability of many people of the West. American Indians, on the other hand, look at reality in a way that makes it possible for them to know something by temporarily turning into it.

That is not as strange as it may seem. Indian oral tradition and the teachings of holy people make it clear that "becoming something else" is not exactly what is meant by the English word "transformation." So I am not trying to convince anybody that the metamorphosis of one thing into another is a possibility in terms of Western realism. But there are other worlds and other realities. People like American Indians, who do not normally make a distinction between dreaming and waking, are capable of a type of projection or transference which they experience as "transformation." It does not matter in the least whether this makes sense to Western mentality any more than it finally matters, for instance, if the writings of Carlos Castaneda are accepted as factual or fictive.

In one memorable episode of the Don Juan tetralogy, an automobile owned by Carlos disappears and reappears. Baffled, the young apprentice asks his Indian teachers if such a mystical event had *really* occurred or if it was simply an illusion. The *brujos* laugh and tell Carlos: "But everything *really* happens!"

That is not an easy conviction for people of the West, for they must believe within the confines of their beliefs. Wallace Stevens understood this dilemma very well when he observed that "reality is not what it is. It consists of the many realities which it can be made into." Transformation is one of the most valuable ways of *making* realities.

Cézanne saw in a tree something more fundamental than what a photo-realist would see. He painted the "treeness" of the tree. In his art he made a living thing out of a teacup, or rather, as Wassily Kandinsky wisely observed, "In a teacup he realized the existence of something alive. . . . He painted these things as he painted human beings, because he was endowed with the gift of divining the inner life in *everything.*"

This visionary capacity of artists is so famous that it is considered by Euro-American standards to be a bit bizarre—and in the dominant society that isn't good. Not since the time of the Byzantines, not since the periods of Romanesque and Gothic sculpture, has the visionary ideal in art held great influence over the naturalism to which the West has been wholly committed. The Renaissance, which took its inspiration almost solely from the idealized expression of the external reality that flourished in Hellenic and Roman art, left little place for alternative realities. Only the genius of painters like El Greco kept the visionary tradition alive and passed it along to Goya in Spain. This rarefied Spanish influence shaped the art of Daumier and Manet; while in the north of Europe it was the visionary imagery of Rembrandt and such contemporaries as Brouwever that stirred the young artists of France, like Delacroix, Decamps, and Courbet; who, in turn, opened the way to the great Cézanne, Gauguin, and Van Gogh.

I do not know if these seminal artists and visionaries were conscious of their capacity to be transformed into the things they painted. But it is certain that they effectively carried a "precivilized" grasp of imagery into the twentieth century.

There are still many people who deny that such visionary art possesses significance. They feel that it is derived almost entirely from an archaic expression that was dictated by nothing but ignorance of the correct, classical methods of representation. They draw analogies between "neo-primitive visionary painters" and the mentality of children. They believe it is absurd for painters to learn from ages when art was, however sincere, "incompetent and uneducated."

"It is no easy matter," the translator of Kandinsky's writings, Michael Sadler, has said, "to conquer the assumption that visionary art and its [primal] antecedents are merely untrained naturalism—undertaken by painters who deliberately reject the knowledge and skills of centuries."

But regardless of the density of Western naturalistic biases, an alternative reality survived in the images of visionary painters to become the dominant idiom of art in the twentieth century. Implicit in that painterly vision is the metaphor, if not the mystic reality, of knowing things by turning into them.

Who can tell the dancer from the dance? (W. B. Yeats)

TRANSFORMATION AS A SOURCE OF IMAGERY

The painter "takes his body with him," says Valéry. French phenomenologist Maurice Merleau-Ponty (1964a) adds to this conviction: "It is by lending his body to the world that the artist changes the world into paintings." These are clearly metaphors for the kind of *transformation* I have been describing. It is the process by which primal people become aware of things. This awareness is also the basis by which Indian painters, like the Sioux who debated with Rudolph Friederich Kurz on the banks of the Yellowstone River, ritualize reality in the form of images.

It is curious that Rodin, who was twelve years old when Kurz visited America in 1852, understood the vision of the Sioux painter far better than the Swiss artist-explorer. "It is the artist who is truthful, while the photograph is mendacious; for, in reality, time never stops cold." The photograph destroys the overtaking, the overlapping, the metamorphosis of time. This is what the images of painting make visible, because, as Rodin explained, "the horse has in him that *leaving here, going there* which is time; because the horse has a foot in each instant. Painting searches not for the outside of movement but for its secret ciphers. All flesh, and even that of the world, radiates beyond itself." These statements are also metaphors of transformation. Rodin became aware of the essential nature of the horse not through naturalistic observation but by becoming the horse.

Merleau-Ponty said: "It is impossible to say that nature ends here and that man or expression starts here." (1964b)

Giotto did not learn painting by looking at live sheep but by studying the sheep painted by Cimabue. The image of art is not a substitute for the original. When we see the Franz Hals portrait of Descartes we should think of Hals and not of Descartes. An image is not a deliberately puzzling sign that points to something else. It means what it is. And to share in its meaning we must become the painting we are seeing, for that is the creative aspect of vision; just as the painter is necessarily transformed into what he is painting by the very process of making images.

For American Indians and other primal peoples this arduous and complex process I have been describing is a way of life. What is called "the creative process" by the West is an effervescence of living for native peoples. Perhaps an Indian holy person said it better: "The apple is a very complicated thing . . . but for the apple tree it is easy."

Phenomenologist Mikel Dufrenne said much the same thing from the Western viewpoint: "For the [primal person], truth does not lie in the insignificant appearances of the everyday world but in the great cosmic forces which course through this world, in the exemplary events recounted in myth and repeated in ritual, and in all that gives meaning to appearances rather than receiving it from them. The same can be said about the totem poles of the Haida Indians [of the Northwest Coast of America], the painted ancestors of the New Hebrides, or the bronze figures of the Steppes. Such works attempt to render the invisible visible." The artist has used his body—his cumulative sensory being—to transform something mysterious into something tangible.

For Indians, images are a means of celebrating mystery and not a manner of explaining it. For Kandinsky art was essentially the same thing: "To speak of mystery in terms of mystery. Is that not content? Is that not the conscious or unconscious *purpose* of the compulsive urge to create?"

Until the age of neuropsychiatry and phenomenology it was perhaps difficult for the Western mind to come to terms with this often restated theme of artists and primal peoples: that reality is multiple and not singular; that we live in a multiverse and not a universe. So intent is the West upon the assumption that behind all occurrences and appearances lies a *singular law* that highly rational people, like scientists, repudiate the multiplicity of their own experience. Psychologist Robert E. Ornstein has pointed out that "many intellectuals are to a certain extent afraid when an intuition intrudes into their thought processes; they are diffident and treat it very gingerly; consciously or unconsciously, in most cases they repress it." Amorphous sensibilities such as intuition, imagination, passivity, sensuality, ambiguity, and holisticy have long been dissociated from the *oneness* of the West and attributed instead to the non-rational and the feminine—both of which are held in very little esteem in Western classicism. But despite the monopolistic dogma that envisions the oneness of God and His universe, a tormented dualism has steadily nagged at the consciousness of Western intellectuals. Rather than consenting to the possibility that truth is nonexistent or pluralistic, they have consented to the very complex and suicidal notion that within the oneness of the truth is an implacable dualism. Consciousness is therefore regarded as a delicate tightrope walk through a lifetime of polarized experiences. The recent right-left brain discoveries have heightened rather than dismissed this idea of a polarity that lies hidden behind the oneness of God. Therefore, Ornstein could say that "it is the polarity and the integration of these two modes of consciousness, the complementary workings of the intellect and the intuition, which underlies our highest achievements"; thus reforming rather than dismissing the compulsive monomania of the West.

There is no question, incidentally, that Dr. Ornstein's statement is intended to liberate the intuitional from its long subservience to reason, but by presuming that the brain's multiplicity is a polarity—a mathematical conception of two halves rather than a nonmathematical organization that is as wondrous as the specialized functions of the parts themselves—he has put us right back into the same paradoxical Western position: one plus one equals One.

Whatever may be the eventual philosophical implications of the right-left brain specialization—which implies that one side of the brain is essentially "rational" while the other is "intuitional"—it seems to me to be extremely naive to assume that even in such a mysterious realm as human consciousness we may impose the equation that one and one equals One, that the integration of two opposites results in the antiquated Western concept of an ultimate oneness.

It is true that Hopi Indians distinguish between the function of the two hands, one for writing and one for making music; and it is also true that Mojave Indians designate the left hand as the passive, mother-side of the person while the right is the active, father-side; but it is entirely mistaken to attribute to Indians the same duality that is the basis of Western thinking. The ultimate reality for the Hopis is *'a'ne himu*—"a mighty something." That is about as ambiguous as you can be in English, but still the words fail to express the multiplicity (and not dualism or mathematical unity) underlying Hopi sensibility. Black Elk expressed a typical Northern Plains Indian attitude when he said: "While I stood there I saw more than I can tell and I understood more than I saw: for I was seeing in a sacred manner the shapes of all things in the spirit, and the shape of all shapes as they must live together like one being."

What is essential about this comment is the word "like"— for when Black Elk says "as they must live together *like* one being," he makes it perfectly clear that for Indians the oneness of consciousness is not an ultimate and fixed reality but a sacred capacity for centeredness, for an integration of the self and the world that is learned. It is a lesson learned through a vision of the unspeakable plurality that transforms the person of wisdom into the shape of all shapes—so that the powers within and around him may live together *like* one being. This integrity is fragile in the Indian world, and its disharmony or disintegration is the cause of disease or death.

The reality implied by Black Elk's statement is as difficult to grasp literally as an ideal metaphor in the writings of the Spanish poet Federico García Lorca:

> . . . occasionally a swarm of coins
> devours abandoned children.

What Black Elk has offered us is a description of the sort of holistic consciousness that is usually alien to the Western viewpoint.

A Zuñi Indian once asked an ethnologist who was meticulously noting each word of a traditional story, "When I tell these stories, do you *see* it, or do you just write it down?"

That question is not nearly as curious as it may seem when taken literally—for it is not a literal question. As Dennis and Barbara Tedlock have perceptively pointed out in their anthology *Teachings from the American Earth*, even in the empirical West there are alternatives to the "single vision" of Newton. William Blake called it "double vision," and by the term, like the Zuñi Indian, he implies not a dualism but a vast alternative access to the multiplicities of experience. "May God keep us from single vision and Newton's sleep," Blake wrote in his *Letter to Thomas Butts*, 1802. Plotinus, the Neo-Platonist of A.D. 250, said something similar: "To any vision must be brought an eye adapted to what is to be seen."

"Otherness" does not imply a single, alternative option but a multiverse of possibilities. When the Zuñi asked the ethnologist if he could *see* the story rather than simply transcribe it in hard-and-fast words, he was asking if a white man were capable of *entering* the story and having the story enter him. He wanted to know if an ethnologist, if a white man, could tell the dancer from the dance—because, if he could somehow make such a dubious distinction, then he would surely fail, from the Zuñi standpoint, to see anything at all.

But we must not assume from this that primal peoples lack a sense of empirical reality and are somehow at sea in a cosmos of endless ambiguities. As Ernst Cassirer (1944) has observed, native peoples have a very pragmatic side as well.

> What is characteristic of [primal] mentality is not its logic but its general sentiment of life. [Primal] man does not look at nature with the eyes of a naturalist who wishes to classify

things in order to satisfy an intellectual curiosity. He does not approach it with merely pragmatic or technical interest. It is for him neither a mere object of knowledge nor the field of his immediate practical needs. We are in the habit of dividing our life into the two spheres of practical and theoretical activity. In this division we are prone to forget that there is a . . . stratum beneath them both. [Primal] man is not liable to such forgetfulness. All his thoughts and his feelings are still embedded in this . . . original stratum. His view of nature is neither merely theoretical nor merely practical; it is *sympathetic*. If we miss this point we cannot find the approach to the mystical world. [Primal] man by no means lacks the ability to grasp the empirical differences of things. But in his conception of nature and life all these differences are obliterated by a stronger feeling: the deep conviction of a fundamental and indelible *solidarity of life* that bridges over the multiplicity and variety of its single forms. He does not ascribe to himself a unique and privileged place in the scale of nature.

The Native American grasp of the *solidarity of life* is an expression of kinship and not a conviction of unity. The *sympathetic* undertone of the relationship of primal peoples to the world around them is ritualized in both empirical and mystical forms. The story that the Zuñi Indian told the ethnologist was a tangible aspect of oral tradition; while the ability to "see" the story, which was so important to the storyteller, is the intangible aspect of the impulse behind the story. Both of these aspects of an image are of equal importance. They are fundamental to an understanding of imagery and the experience of "seeing" in the primal sense.

Before we discuss the concrete forms in which images become visible in Indian painting I want to make a few more observations about the significance of "seeing" from the primal viewpoint. Without these remarks and those which have been under discussion here, we cannot readily translate Indian iconography and visions into terms that make realis-

tic sense to the Western mind. Without these insights the reality of Indians fails to become a metaphor and remains exotic and alien—and thus the "mighty something" of which
the West is so tragically bereft cannot be reinfused into
Western consciousness, and we cannot find within each of
us the precious otherness that makes us divine and human.

> It may be that some little root of the sacred tree still lives.
> Nourish it then, that it may leaf and bloom and fill with
> singing birds.   (BLACK ELK)

"WHO SPEAKS TO ME WITH MY OWN VOICE?"

Representation is a complex and infinitely various relationship between reality and the symbols used to depict it. The
mili, representing the breath-of-life given to the world by
Awonawilona, the "mighty something" of the Zuñi, is envisioned as a perfect ear of corn, filled with seeds of sacred
plants, wrapped in buckskin, set in a base of basketry, and
covered with feathers from various birds. This *mili* is the embodiment of something unspeakable. It is more significant
than any of the physical things that compose it. It contains a
living force which, if treated properly and with respect and
if ceremonially fed, will give power to its owners. Such an
object may be owned by an individual or by a clan, by a secret society, or by an entire tribe. The Corn Mother of the
Hako Ceremony of the Pawnee, for instance, is owned by
the tribe. The visionary images painted on a Blackfeet shield,
however, are personal powers given to the person who
painted and possesses them. Because such images are living
forces, they must be cared for and ceremonially fed, usually
with cornmeal in the American Southwest and with tobacco
smoke in the Great Plains. When not in use, images are usually kept in special containers and in special places. They
must be protected.

Images, such as the *mili* of the Zuñi, can be symbolical in

such a specific way that they might be called ideographs—
images that relate to ideas and emotions. A similar use of
thought-scribing can be seen taking shape in the pictographic language of the Chinese. The pictograph for eye and the
one for water were combined to become the pictograph for
weeping. This kind of image-making seems to have been familiar to most American Indian tribes. In the Great Lakes region there are pictographs made on birch bark. In the Plains
there are animal skins that were used as the medium for pic-
ture-writing. Across the entire Northern Hemisphere there
are pictographs and petroglyphs painted and incised on
boulders, cliff faces, and cave walls.

This so-called rock art exists in great variety—sometimes
having the appearance of feet and crosses, sometimes taking
on animal forms. There is an abundance of checkerboard
patterns and lines that zigzag and parallel each other with
what appears to be a meaningful repetition. Birds, insects,
and images of the sun appear frequently.

There is, among Western scholars, a great deal of debate
on the subject of whether these images were *art* in even the
remotest sense of what is meant by that word in the West,
for one scribe often placed his icons directly over those
painted earlier by another; and none of these "artists" had
any apparent attitude about how images should be spatially
arranged on a surface. There is also debate about whether
these were simply pictographs (representations of things) or
if they had been conceptually broadened into some form of
ideographs (representations of ideas about things). Some of
these images on rock faces predate the arrival of Columbus
while others were produced as recently as the end of the
nineteenth century, but no one survives who knows for certain the Indian's original understanding of the imagery.

There is an inclination among Western researchers to
want to see this rock art as ideographic writing, since such a
representational use of images would affirm that Indians

were retardedly moving in the same direction as the West and the Orient. But we will probably never know with certainty the significance of the thousands of images painted and incised across the North American continent.

Such pictographs and ideographs are quite different from written languages based on phonetic symbols. This sound-writing is by no means universal among the peoples of the world, but among those who use it, there are two major forms: the alphabetic and the syllabic. The syllabary, which depicts sounds in syllables, formulates the symbols or letters associated with every consonant attached to every vowel: aa-ae-ai-ao-au, ba-be-bi-bo-bu, etc. This is a syllabary, and it was the form which the Cherokee Indian named Sequoya partly rediscovered and partly invented for writing the language of his people. The second form of sound-writing, the alphabetical system, is familiar to Western people because their languages are expressed in it: a sign or letter stands for each individual sound of the language. In the West two Semitic peoples—the Hebrews and the Phoenicians—first used the alphabetic form of written language.

For Orientals who possess an alternative concept of writing and for primal peoples who entrust their ideas and history to oral tradition rather than written documents, the form and content of Western language is mysterious. A culture's mode of thought is not only illustrated but also limited by the manner of its speech and writing. There have been many different cultural solutions to communication, each perfectly formulated for its expressive ends. This is perhaps the ultimate miracle of humanity—its great expressive variety and diversity.

One of the most startling discoveries of learning a language totally unrelated to the one spoken in our homes is the manner in which words (and images) are used to voice subtly different attitudes and modes of thought. Take, for example, the language of the Wintu Indians of northern California. There is no nominal plural form among these people, and when they do use a plural word, such as *men*, they use a root completely different from the singular word: man is *wita* but men is *gis*. As Dorothy Lee commented in *Freedom and Culture:* "To someone brought up in the Indo-European tradition, this is a position hard to understand. We know that the plural is derived from the singular. It is logical and natural for our grammars to start with the singular form of a noun or a verb, and then go on to the plural." But to a Wintu Indian it is equally natural to speak of deer or salmon without any distinction in regard to number. To a member of this tribe a flock or a herd is a singular whole; it is not a collection of individual elements. To Western people the distinction of number is so essential to their thinking that they do not mention an object without also indicating whether it is singular or plural; and if they refer to it in the present tense, the verb always reflects the number. When Dorothy Lee asked a Wintu the word for "body" she was given a term meaning *the whole person*. The Wintu does not say *my head aches;* he says *I head ache*.

"There is for the Wintu a premise of a reality beyond his delimiting experience," Lee states.

> His experience is that of a reality shaped by his perception and conceptualization. Beyond it is the timeless design to which his experience has given temporality. He believes in it, and he taps it through his ritual acts and his magic, seeking luck to reinforce and validate his experiential skills and knowledge, to endow his acts with effectiveness. A hunter must have both skill and luck; but skill is the more limited. An unskilled hunter who has luck, can still hit a deer by rare chance, but a skilled hunter without luck can never do so. The myths contain examples of hunters who, having lost their luck, can never kill a deer again. Now knowledge and

skill are phrased agentively and experientially; but luck is phrased passively or in terms of non-actualized reality. The hunter who has lost his luck does not say "I cannot kill deer any more," but "Deer don't want to die for me any more."

In grasping the way in which many primal peoples formulate images, it is necessary to understand how they see themselves in relation to the world, since images are a result of concepts of perception. Indians do not address nature as underlings nor do they command. Their participation in the world is symbiotic to such an extent that they discover nature within and outside of themselves.

"Recurring through all this is the attitude of humility and respect toward reality, toward nature and society," Dorothy Lee observes.

> I cannot find an adequate English term to apply to a habit of thought which is so alien to our culture. We are aggressive toward reality. We say, *This is bread*; we do not say like the Wintu, *I call this bread.* . . . If he speaks of reality which is not within his own restricting experience, he does not affirm it, he only implies it. If he speaks of his experience, he does not express it as categorically true. Our attitude toward nature is colored by a desire to control and exploit. The Wintu relationship with nature is one of intimacy and mutual courtesy. He kills a deer only when he needs it for his livelihood, and utilizes every part of it, hoofs and marrow and hide and sinew and flesh. Waste is abhorrent to him, not because he believes in the intrinsic virtue of thrift, but because the deer had died for him.

IMAGE INTO RITUAL AND ART

Indians of North America produced an elaborate oral tradition but no written languages. They did devise a number of practical memory aids. Notches were made on sticks as memory links, standing for events in the oral history entrusted to a tribal memory specialist. The notches were like multiple "strings tied around his fingers," reminding him not of one thing but of a succession of things. The Papago Indians of Arizona had Calendar-Stick Men who had the ability to feel the notches on the sticks and thus be reminded by each notch, or perhaps the combination of notches, of an event that they would then elaborate and recite. Conceptually such devices are entirely remote from the languages of the West, and yet they represent an element of primal imagery. The notches, like the beading of the original wampum of the Northeastern region, were not "shorthand" nor any other form of writing. They were secret pores into a knowledge that lay in the memories—in the bodies—of a whole people and not in their signs or writings. Nor were these mnemonic devices the sort of practical notations used in the earliest Western civilizations, such as the Eurasian cultures which invented writing essentially for keeping accounts and similar utilitarian purposes. It is far more likely that they are visual metaphors: the *images* in which primal peoples conduct conversations with "a mighty something" within them and all around them.

I was once given advice by an Indian who was very much worried about my preoccupation with words. "You must learn to look at the world twice," he told me as I sat on the floor of his immaculately swept adobe room. "First you must bring your eyes together in front so you can see each droplet of rain on the grass, so you can see the smoke rising from an anthill in the sunshine. *Nothing* should escape your notice. But you must learn to look again, with your eyes at the very edge of what is visible. Now you must see dimly if you wish to see things that are dim—visions, mist, and cloud-people ...animals which hurry past you in the dark. You must learn to look at the world twice if you wish to see all that there is to see."

The ability to envision a second world is a major source of

knowledge . . . that which is so deeply known and felt, so primal in form that it is neither word nor outcry, neither sign nor symbol—but the ineffable *thing* itself; that which precedes speech and thought, that which is the raw experience itself without evaluation or judgments. It is the ineffable, structured into images. And what, after all, is this mysterious iconography that has eluded the Western mind for centuries, and why have I spent so much time discussing it as a prerequisite for understanding the Indian use of imagery? It is an appearance—an apparition, if you like—that springs not from what we are, but from what we experience in our perpetual exchange with nature. When you see an image you do not merely see what is physically before you. What you see is an interaction of forces by which something else arises. Those who see only what is before them are blind to many of the events of reality. Primal images, like all art, require us *really* to see. What we are able to see if we are capable of using our bodies as eyes is a virtual image. It is real, for when we are confronted by it, it really does exist, but it is not actually there. The reflection in a mirror is such a virtual image; so is a rainbow. It seems to stand on earth or in the clouds, but it really "stands" nowhere. It is only visible, not tangible. It is the unspeakable, the ineffable made visible, made experiential.

When Wintu Indians use the term *the whole person* to designate the English word "body" they are speaking out of a tradition that perfectly grasps the body as a spiritual instrument. The term of the Wintu possesses physicality—which is the *only* connotation of "body" to the Western mind—but it also possesses a multiplicity of virtual—apparitional and transformational—facilities that are unrecognized in the realism of the West. Ever since the decline of the ecstatic mystery rites of pre-Socratic Greece and the later (third and fourth centuries A.D.) Mediterranean cults of Cybele, Ma, Isis, and Mithras, Western civilization has been continually challenged by its dream of escaping its framework: the categorical, the linear, and the eternally fixed and knowable.

The Western scheme, in the view of many critics, has brought the impulse to express feelings too rigidly under the domination of reason, and this, in turn, has caused Western people to think of themselves predominantly as perpetual spectators of the world—standing somehow outside of nature yet governed by "natural law." Until very recently, most people of the West were completely cut off from their own bodies by the residue of a religious constraint and by embarrassment. They lacked a body that could function in harmony with their ideas and feelings and experiences: they lacked, in effect, what the Wintu Indians call *the whole person*. Consequently they devised a metaphysical standard that placed everything outside of their bodies, away and at a distance. They confirmed the objects and events of the world in languages that speak of experience as categorically true: *This is bread*. The intrinsic aggression of such a viewpoint destroys the apparitional aspects of art and reality generally, since it is incapable of symbiosis. It cannot *participate* in other beings and objects but can only observe them. Without an *articulate body*, without a sense of the body's wholeness, we cannot participate in the world that lies beyond observation—in art and in the minds of primal peoples.

Perhaps it now becomes clear how and why the iconography of American Indians is the apparition of forces that cannot be designated in linear and aggressive languages, nor assigned an external existence entirely removed from our wholeness as persons.

Indian objects, which are often elaborately covered with images, are not in the slightest decorative, at least not in the same sense as a European teacup, for instance, painted with roses presumably to disguise the fact that it is a teacup. The objects of Indians are expressive and not decorative because they are alive, living in our experience of them. When the

Indian potter collects clay, she asks the consent of the river-
bed and sings its praises for having made something as
beautiful as clay. When she fires her pottery, to this day, she
still offers songs to the fire so it will not discolor or burst her
wares. And, finally, when she paints her pottery, she imprints it with the images that give it life and power—because for an Indian, pottery is something significant, not just
a utility but a "being" for which there is as much of a natural order as there is for persons or foxes or trees. So reverent
is the Indian conception of the "power" within things, and
especially the objects created by traditional craftspeople, that
among many Indians the pottery interred with the dead has
a small perforation, a "kill-hole," made in the center in order
to release the *orenda*—the "spiritual power"—before it is
buried.

There are many sources in American Indian lives for the
images that appear on rock surfaces, on the adobe walls of
underground ceremonial chambers, on pottery, altarboards,
masks, shields, tipi linings, and the complex patterns of
body paintings. One of the most pervasive experiences that
brings about such personal or tribal images is the apparition
of the vision quest.

THE WAYS OF IMAGERY

August 1870: it is night. The Blackfeet Indian Wolf Collar
is unconscious, perhaps struck by lightning. Thunder, first
as a bird, then a woman, takes him into her tipi and gives
him a drum and four songs. She gives him power to heal
people struck by lightning: "You must rub a mixture of yellow paint and wet clay on the person's chest and sing the
songs."

She then tells him he may paint upon his tipi the images
imprinted upon her Blue Thunder Lodge. So it was that he
painted a yellow Thunderbird on his blue Thunder tipi. On

the drum he painted a blue Thunderbird, against a yellow background. Later that same night Wolf Collar dreams again. Iron Voice, the Young Thunder, says to him: "I am the one that strikes. I am going to make a great holy man of you; and you will surprise your people. I will come many times when you are sleeping, each time teaching you something new." Then Young Thunder gives Wolf Collar a shield and two songs.*

This experience of Wolf Collar in 1870 would normally be described as hallucination or dream. Such terms have overtones of illusion, phantasmagoria, and deception in the West. Parents in the dominant culture comfort their children when they awaken from dreams by telling them that "the dream was not real." They do not consider the third of our lifetime spent asleep as part of reality. The West has no cultural mechanisms for allowing dreams to substantially enter into and shape experience.

Primal peoples have quite a different view of dream and hallucination. Ethnologist Kilton Stewart, who has done a great deal of dream research among the peoples of various cultures, reports that the Senoi of Malaya instruct their children how to enter actively into and shape their dreams. He feels strongly that the failure to recognize nonfactual experience as an intrinsic part of consciousness is a major failing of the West. Carl Jung championed a broader and more complex cause, and is perhaps the person in this century most responsible for widening the Western conception of the significance of the whole scope of human consciousness. His research into dream analysis is legendary.

Despite this gradual reconstruction of the Western distrust of nonmaterial experience, it was still exceedingly difficult to speak of any kind of extraordinary event, appearance, or action without apologizing for it by calling it a dream or a hal-

---

* Based on the account of Ted Brasser, "Wolf Collar: The Shaman as Artist."

lucination. Naturalistic literature is filled with countless examples of marvelous tales that compulsively conclude with
the narrator awakening to discover that it was "all a dream."
Only in myths and fairy tales are we exempt in the West
from the necessity of justifying "the impossible." The rebirth of a visionary literature, however—like that of Franz
Kafka, Jakov Lind, William Faulkner, Kurt Vonnegut, Jr.,
Gabriel García Marquez, Jorge Luis Borges, among many
others—has undertaken the gradual reeducation of Western
sensibility and, in combination with the soft-drug adven-
tures and misadventures of the 1960s generation, has resulted in a liberated, if sometimes cultish, respect for the unlimited bounds of human experience. It is therefore easier today
than ever before in contemporary Western history to speak
of the Native American vision quest in terms of a psychological realism, if not a reality bounded by the material
world.

With all of this in mind, the story told by Wolf Collar may
be seen as a vital series of psychological revelations that had
a profound and lasting impact upon his life. His visions (images) are the equivalent of the startling "inspirations" and
"intuitions" that artists and scientists describe as the sudden
and marvelous sources of their most brilliant ideas and discoveries. French phenomenologist Mikel Dufrenne said:
"The imagination is that which is least human in man." It
wrenches him away from himself and plunges him into ec-
stasy; it puts him into secret communion with the powers of
nature. "Who speaks to me, with my own voice?" From himself comes a marvelous stranger called Art.

Because Wolf Collar and primal people like him have not
closed themselves off from the nonmaterial aspects of experience, his "intuition" is capable of existing as apparition, as
virtual image . . . a *substance* independent of materiality.
Here we are clearly entering an entirely different cosmos
from the one in which the West exists. We must cease speak-

ing of "reality" as if it were necessarily ordinary. We must deautomatize consciousness in order to approach that celebrated pronouncement of William Blake: "If the doors of perception were cleansed, man would see everything as it is, infinite." And yet we must somehow manage to do this without falling back upon occultism, which is simply the same old Western apology for the extraordinary, excusing it by calling it "dream" or "supernatural." There is absolutely nothing "mystical"—in the popular and very negative sense of that term—in the notion that *everything* that happens to us, everything we think, everything we envision, imagine, conceive, perceive, dream, and intuit, is a real and vital part of our lives. And it is at the very least in this metaphoric frame of mind (if we cannot manage to discard all limits placed upon reality) that we must try to grasp the experiences of peoples from drastically different worlds than ours in the West.

The individual experience of images and ideas is for almost all Indians of the Americas a communion with the "mighty something" that is the abiding power of the cosmos. Much as all creative people depend upon intuition or inspiration for their life-supporting and life-affirming discoveries and imaginings, Indians depend upon some sort of personal contact with the ineffable for their most precious wisdom. But consistent with the primal willingness to visualize or to imagine experience holistically rather than carefully restrict its existence to a material realm, Indians understand their contact with the unspeakable in a ritualized form so that it takes the *real* shapes of beings that anthropologists usually call "spirit-helpers." Although the importance of such spirit-helpers differs considerably from area to area in the Western Hemisphere, they exist in virtually every region of the Americas. This contact of an individual with cosmic powers is extraordinary from the Western perspective, insofar as such contact in the West is normally restricted to an initiated and somewhat secretive priesthood. By comparison, spiritual power is usually highly individuated among Indians.

Such personal experience of the "mighty something" is not as democratic among the masonry civilizations of Mexico and Central America. Likewise, among the Pueblo Indians of the American Southwest, as well as other localities where there is a sedentary, agricultural lifestyle and an organized priesthood, visionary experiences are largely confined to the specialists much as they are in the Western world. By contrast, the vision quest is of supreme value among the Indians of the Plains, where a hunting and nomadic culture lent a decided individuation to the Native American mentality. Generally, however, Indians are encouraged to make contact both individually and as a group with the underlying spiritual powers of the cosmos. Every adult Indian tends to agree that the basis of success in life is much dependent upon not only one's own efforts, but also the symbiotic relationship with forces that put the individual and the tribe in touch with the "mighty something."

This fundamental power is normally designated by anthropologists as a "pantheistic and animistic belief in a primal world force which exists in all things," but as D. H. Lawrence, in his famed writings about the Southwest (*The Vast Old Religion of Taos*, 1936), perceptively noted: "It was a vast old religion, greater than anything we know: more darkly and nakedly religious. There is no God, no conception of a god. All is god. But it is not the pantheism we are accustomed to, which expresses itself as 'God is everywhere, God is in everything.' In this Indian religion everything is alive, not supernaturally but naturally alive."

The Indian name of this fundamental life force is called *orenda*, from the Iroquois name of the energy inherent in everything in the cosmos. The *orendas* of the innumerable beings and objects are greatly different from one another and require different actions by which people may remain in a positive relationship with them. Therefore a great variety of ceremonies, songs, and rites are used to retain harmony with this awesome power, which is the basis of everything that exists. Corresponding to the Iroquoian *orenda* is the *wakanda* of the Dakota (Sioux) people, the Algonquian *manito*, the Shoshonean *pokunt*, and the Athabascan *coen*. The visions, the *images*, the spirit-helpers that arise from dream and hallucination put the individual in contact with the *orenda*, manifesting it and strengthening it within that "dreamer" so he or she might live and prosper rather than decline and die.

Very often the *orenda* appears in the form of an animal, but this is not surprising when we consider that the Indian generally thinks of animals as possessing superior powers to man, for Indians do not consider themselves the center of the cosmos or the special creatures intended to dominate the world. The Native Americans of North America, in particular, do not think of their relationship to nature as special, and therefore they do not believe themselves to be a "chosen people" (as the Aztec of Mexico did); nor do they believe themselves responsible to powers or divinities to make great sacrifices and payments for the good lives they lead. There is a marked difference between most North American Indian cultures and those of Mexico, Peru, and Europe, where sacrifice was usually involved in every form of ceremony. The relationship between the Indian and the *orendas* has always been drastically different from what it is in most other cultures. Among Indians there is far more emphasis upon a friendly exchange than on the kind of supplication and humility that marks most religious rites. Offerings are not made in the form of sacrifices, nor, for that matter, can they really be called "gifts." Instead, they are tokens that recall the relationship of equals and of spiritual friends. Except for the possible prehistoric emphasis in the Near East on animal ancestors and the free exchange between men and spirits of

Egypt (which resulted in animal divinities in eras predating the organized priesthood), there is nothing in Western civilization that quite parallels the *orendas* of American Indians. In the initiation from childhood to maturity, no experience is as important to Indians in at least half the geographical regions of North America as the gaining of a spirit-helper in a vision quest. Without it a person would surely fail in every major activity of life. So Indians do not usually await the appearance of some aspect of the *orenda*, but actively seek it. This is the basis of the vision quest. Such quests often begin as early as the fifth year of either a boy or a girl, though it is usually the traditional undertaking of puberty that marks the initiation into adult life.

In the old days, a young person traveled to some remote area where it was known that many powers dwelled—often a mountaintop, or the shore of a remote lake, sometimes in the depths of a deep forest. There the youth remained for several days and nights, alone and in utter silence, fasting from both food and water, humbly naked except for a loincloth since for most Indians the body is all a person owns, sometimes offering flesh from the arms or legs and otherwise enduring hardships that provoked hallucination.

As Peter Farb has pointed out, this belief in visions existed almost universally among Indians of North America, but it seems to have evolved into two distinctive forms. "Among some Indians it led directly to shamanism, for shamans were believed to be recipients of particularly intense visions and to have the power of summoning up new visions at will. The other line of development led to visions of more limited power that had to be sought after. A great range of variation occurred in this second category—from the Plains youth, who suffered ordeals, to the Great Basic Shoshone, who passively waited for the spirit to find him." In most cases, however, fasting, sleeplessness, and other forms of hardship were the major means of stimulating visions. It must be remembered that in primeval North America the Plains tribes had made remarkably little use of plants such as peyote, certain mushrooms, jimsonweed, and other such hallucinogens. Nor, as Farb indicates, "had the Plains tribes learned that tobacco, which they smoked for a few ritual puffs, when swallowed could produce considerable discomfort and emotional upheaval, as it did in many Central and South American Indians" in search of visions. Only after about 1850, when the Plains culture was rapidly disintegrating, did the hallucinogenic cactus known as peyote take hold as an access to vision and an escape from the humiliation of military defeat.

The young people in search of a vision in the days prior to 1850 relied upon sacred songs and hardship to bring them into contact with the *orendas*. If a youth was fortunate he or she would be approached by a vision that usually took the form of both visual and auditory hallucinations. An animal-power would appear and speak to the neophyte, teaching a song or revealing secret and powerful images that he or she was instructed to paint on the body, clothing, shield, and tipi as a manifestation of personal power.

When returning to his or her people, the youth would describe the experience to close friends and relations, reconstructing it and filling in gaps, adapting it to the mythic norms of the culture. Often the vision, the songs, and the images given to the neophyte were kept secret for a lifetime, until, in old age, they were passed along to a deserving apprentice or to someone who was luckless enough not to have ever experienced a vision of his or her own. Even today successful visions support people for their entire lives. It is a power upon which they can call for guidance and courage. During the vision, the youth is usually told what things must be collected for a sacred bundle, wrapped in animal skin, which is carefully kept as a symbolic embodiment of the power that guides one's life and gives protection and good fortune.

Much of the "art" of American Indians is not art in the formal Western sense at all, but the careful representation of the iconography given to a person during a vision quest, or given in the dreams of later life. These emblems and images are materialized and used in pottery, textile, paintings, and carvings. Whether tribally or individually owned, the power of these images is what makes them significant and not simply their aesthetic impact upon those who do not not know or understand the metaphor underlying their imagery. It is here, in this emblematic and visionary realm, that all art of the world finally possesses its vividness and power. We have reconstructed the vision implicit in art as an image conforming to the norms of our cultures, mindless of the fact that we have thus transformed a ritualistic experience into something called "art" in an effort to convey an unspeakable revelation within the confines of our closed concept of reality. As a vision often divorced from its motivating power, decorative art is a dubious achievement in the West, but for Native Americans, even when their art-making has been highly influenced by Western media and techniques, the *orendas* remain the central and essential impulse behind images.

Perhaps it is now clear in retrospect why the meeting of Rudolph Friederich Kurz and a Sioux Indian artist on the banks of the Yellowstone River in 1852 was such a revealing cultural confrontation. The Indian objected to a scheme of reality that ignored the "fact" that people have two legs and emphasized the "idea" that one person standing in one location would not be able to see the second leg of a rider because the body of the horse would obscure it. The whole notion that images necessarily result from the perspective of one person standing in one location and looking at one object or scene (like the lens of a camera) was entirely alien to the Indian conception of *images*. There is no "power" in this Western idea of perception—no glimpse of the *orendas*, no transformation of the body into an organ of perception. From the Indian viewpoint there is only a rather aimless kind of cartography in this kind of art.

The impulse behind Indian images has little concern for particularization and appearance. Even when the visions of individuals provide the iconography for the design painted upon pottery or woven into textile, still the imagery is visionary rather than decorative or representational. Whether the paintings are the tribal icons of clans or the personally owned images of hunters, pottery-makers, or warriors, whether they are the ancient imprints on the walls of ceremonial chambers, on altarboards and shields, or if they are the images of the Winter Counts by which some tribes kept pictographic history—in all of these instances the imagery remains spiritual in the purest sense of the term. And this spirituality, at least from the standpoint of artists like Wassily Kandinsky, is the basis for our most precious conception of art.

Surely painters such as Kandinsky grasped much of the otherness of primal art and attempted within the bounds of Western interpretation to reinfuse their work with a nearly lost visionary power. Yet this discussion of "image" in the primal mentality has perhaps underscored the probability that much of the art produced by so-called Neo-Primitivists was a superficial reflection of the surface of primal imagery (a kind of plagiarism of appearances), rather than a realization of its underlying reality as the evocation of human dream and memory.

While many masterful artists of the West successfully used primal art to redirect their works in revolutionary and sublime new directions, the *orendas* of the primal mind remained largely lost to them and could not shine from their art. For all the truly brilliant rebelliousness of Cubism and Futurism, and the refusal to accept the linear perspective of Giotto as absolute, the analytical and sequential dogma of the West was every bit as much in evidence in their alternatives to Giotto's painterly cosmos as it was in Giotto's own paintings. Cubism, after all, does not abandon the sequential conception of seeing; it only places more cameras around the same object. The simultaneous point of view of primal art deals not with the "eye as a camera," so to speak, but with the "mind's eye" that consummates everything we know, imagine, feel, conceive, perceive, and dream about an object we are painting. Transformation lets us take our bodies with us into the visionary realm. Transformation relinquishes the point of view of the camera and provides us with direct, physical contact with the *orendas* which appear to us as visions, inspirations, intuitional insights.

When we look at the native illustrations of the codices of the Aztecs or the elaborate painted-histories made by Amos Bad Heart Buffalo, we see before us an elaborate array of visual conventions built upon a concept of "seeing" entirely different from the one understood in the West. This unique image of the Indian mind springs from the total and innermost consciousness of a people, and, if we can learn to grasp its message, we have managed to slip past ourselves and the stern sentries of our cultural isolation, and we have been able to peer momentarily into a reflection of ourselves from the *other side*. As a friend of mine once said: they open up the real with the abstract, giving us a quick look inside before the door slams shut. And in this way, that solitary person within each of us realizes for just a moment that he or she is not alone.

4

TIME

> Events or processes transmitted through oral traditions tend
> to be recounted neither in terms of time past or time future in
> a lineal sense. Indeed most native languages have no such
> tenses to express this. They speak rather of a perennial reality
> of the now.
>
> —JOSEPH EPES BROWN

Primal people are supernaturalists, and for them time is extraordinary. Among the Australian aborigines, for example, there is both the immediate and ordinary time of daily existence as well as an experience they call "dreamtime"—which includes not only the events of our sleeping state but also those things we anticipate, envision, imagine, intuit, and conceive. The aboriginal "dreamtime" is the solution to the Western question asked by the late Hannah Arendt: "Where are we when we think?" It is a question answered without even being asked.

Dreamtime is sacred time—the realm of myth and inspiration. It is the time in which creation takes place, in which the ineffable continuum of nature flickers brightly. It is the reverberation of first things in which the cosmos makes its most ancient drummings, like the genesis depicted by the Quiché Maya in their saga, the *Popol Vuh:*

> The surface of the earth was not yet made. There was only
> the quietude of water and a vast expanse of blue sky. There
> was nothing yet brought together, nothing which could
> make a sound, nor anything which might tremble or gesture
> or sigh. Not in the sky nor in the water was there breathing

or dreaming. There was nothing standing; only the calm sea, the motionless water, alone within itself and silent. Nothing yet existed. There was only a tireless immobility and a perpetual stillness in the vast and deep darkness of the night.

This mythic antiquity of the dreamtime, however, is not truly found in the past as the West understands it. "The rich mythic accounts of creation," Joseph Epes Brown writes, "are not so much of chronological time-past as they usually tend to be read by us. Rather they tell of processses which are of eternal happening; the same processes are recurring now and are to recur in other cycles." Given this structure of experience, supported by primal forms of language, and made immediate by the experience of people's natural environment, it is impossible to conceive of *progress* in the contemporary non-Indian lineal sense in Native American thought. We in the West refer to the cumulative process in which the more and the "new" automatically become identified with the better. Primal people do not conceive of such progressive and secular time. For them time is sacred.

The Western world fails visibly to respond to forces that were exerted in the time of its ancestors. Nevertheless, the reverberation of the dreamtime persists. It is elusive enough to require the name "poetry" in the West and it is immaterial enough to escape the notice of those for whom materiality is supreme . . . but it still exists. "Thus man, in his human time, subsists also in a kind of surviving dreamtime which is eternal and unchanging," Loren Eiseley has stated. "Both men and animals come and go through the generations a little like actors slipping behind the curtain, in order to reappear later, drawn through the totemic center to precisely similar renewed roles in society. Sacred time is of another and higher dimension than secular time. It is, in reality, timeless; past and future are contained within it." All of primal peoples' meaningful relationship to their world is thus not history, not causality in a scientific sense, but a mythical ordering of life that has not deviated and will not in the future deviate from the traditions of immediacy.

In discussing Native American oral literature, Margot Astrov has indicated that to the various Pueblo peoples—and to the Hopi in particular—the phenomena of what the West calls "the objective side of the world" are intimately interlocked with those of the subjective side of experience. Not only do these two apparent polarities interlock and sustain each other holistically, but the subjective realm is apt to dominate the objective connotation of the world. This visionary mode of thought unique to many primal people, the so-called subjective aspect of consciousness, determines their reality.

The force of Native American literature arises from its unaltered emergence from dreamtime and not simply in its empirical observations—and not simply in its potent mythic metaphors. Thus the power of native literature is not discovered in holy words and incantations alone nor in the depiction of extraordinary events alone. The teller's or writer's story is a means of raising one's self to a higher level of achieved power (a concept demonstrated by Carlos Castaneda in his Don Juan books). It is a method of producing the *perpetual reality of the now*. It is a catalyst of time and space that brings from one dimension of experience (dreamtime) the elements that are lost to the materiality of the secular kind of temporal experience. There is for these reasons no more vivid means of discussing the nature of time among primal peoples than through the examination of their grasp of events, histories, characters, and what—ultimately—the West calls literature. Likewise, there is nothing that better contrasts the materiality of Western mentality with the visionary mentality of primal peoples than the way each recreates experience as literature.

THE MATERIALITY OF WESTERN TIME

There are a great many preconceptions with which various societies grasp the world and make it comprehensible, but in the West there is perhaps no single idea as obsessive as the notion of the material reality of time. It is therefore exceedingly difficult to discuss alternative ways of looking at time—sequence, causality, succession, etc.—without confronting this inflexible dogma. As any imaginative writer who has deviated from the naturalism of Zola is well aware, most editors have an insistent attitude about how a story or a novel should be constructed: how one event must follow a prior event, how characters must develop psychologically and motivationally from a past history to a current circumstance, how these characters must be moved from one place to another, how the hours, days, and weeks must flow in a steady, consistent, clear, and directional stream—the future turning into the present and the present turning into the past—each kept in its tidy, linear compartment of time and space. Even in an era revolutionized by Einstein's theory of relativity, a century presumably altered by the thrust of books by Kafka, Joyce, Woolf, and Proust; in a decade which applauds the cinematic abstractions of Antonioni and Resnais, still an author such as Kurt Vonnegut, Jr. must defend himself and his style by declaring that he does not supply his characters with "transportation."

"I do not move them from one room to another; I do not send them up the stairs; they do not get dressed in the mornings; they do not put the ignition key in the lock, and turn on the engine, and let it warm up, and look at all the gauges, and put the car in reverse, and back out, and drive to the filling station, and ask the guy there about the weather. You can fill up a good-sized book with this kind of connective tissue. People are very satisfied with it, too. But I don't do it."

Vonnegut implies that authors, like modern painters and sculptors, are working with a mentality similar to the visionary dreamtime of primal peoples. He also suggests that it is not the task of literature simply to inform or to depict self-contained and significant events, but also to induce in the reader a rarefied performance of the imagination. "No other art requires the audience to be a performer. You have to count on the reader's being a good performer, and yet you may write 'music' which he absolutely can't perform—in which case it's a bust. Some writers are teaching an audience how to play this kind of 'music' in their heads."

Many aspects of postnaturalistic Western literature recapitulate fundamental qualities of native oral literature (and its contemporary, written forms). We might assume that such visionary elements have been fully assimilated by the contemporary Western reader—but as Anaïs Nin insisted, the West is still extremely uncomfortable with anything but literary naturalism. Whereas the experimentation of early twentieth-century painters has been fully amalgamated into Western society—to such an extent that shops offer Cubistic wallpapers—the explorations of literary innovators have had extremely little impact on the methods used in writing magazines and newspapers (where H. L. Mencken is still king) or novels (where the style of Henry James remains more or less mandatory). The public is probably more reactionary in its expectations of literature than of any other contemporary art form.

When we grasp the empirical conception of time in the West we begin to understand the popular resistance to temporal experiments in fiction. At the same time, examples from Western avant-garde literature help us to recognize the process by which the dreamtime of primal peoples is ritualized in their experience.

"The clock," Robert Ornstein has written, "is the very embodiment of linearity and sequence. Inside a clock, the rotation of a wheel or the vibrations of a tuning fork are mechanically translated into movements of a pointer. These yield seconds, then minutes, then hours, one hour follows another, in a strict unchanging sequence." This consistent linear succession of time is so much an intrinsic part of Western consciousness that it seems a bit strange to discuss or to examine its basis and its presumptions. The Western person cannot conceive of an alternative to the successive notion of time. Is it possible that time could operate in any other manner?

The Western way of experiencing time is only one particular construction of reality. There is nothing absolute or final about clocks. Many civilizations have existed without the clock as the West knows it; and without the Western precept of time. To designate clock-time as "real time" is the same as calling American money "real money."

The Western grasp of time is pervasive, making itself visible in the way languages are constructed and the way people are required to arrange their thoughts in a recognizable sequence—even when this requires them to alter their special experiences (such as dreams) in order to fit them into the acceptable temporal framework. It is imperative in the West to falsify our consciousness so it fits the stream of duration that carries us out of the past and into the future. The modality is linear and it is composed equally of a past, present, and future through which a sequence of enduring events follow one another in an orderly and calculable manner.

So unconditional is the Western insistence upon linear time that efforts have been made to postulate some sort of biological basis for its dogmatic sense of time. Diverse processes such as heart rate and basal metabolism have been offered as the source of the Western experience of time. But experiments have shown that these processes referred to as "body clocks" operate at different rates, and no single internal process that could be the ultimate clock has been found.

There are, of course, many internal rhythmic processes important to consciousness, but these do not necessarily relate to time as it is experienced in the West.

Regardless of numerous arguments against the postulation of a bodily organ (a "biological clock") that presumably provides us with our sense of time, many scientists have continued to search for an internal organ of duration. And despite the fact that Western temporal experience is widely regarded by scholars as personally and relativistically constructed, there remains a dominant inclination to view clock-time as absolute. Recently, for example, a group of Midwestern farmers who opposed the introduction of Daylight Saving Time in their region summarized their position by pointing out that "the extra hour of sunlight will burn the grass."

On a more intellectual level the phenomenon of time-experience is crucial to that empirical and observational philosophy called science in the West. Ornstein said: "Causality can be inferred only within a linear mode of temporal consciousness. The information-processing of this mode breaks the flow of events into serial lists which can be sequentially analyzed, studied, and manipulated. Succession and duration are the underpinnings of causality, for without a concept of past and future, of discrete events following each other temporally, it would be impossible to perform scientifically meaningful analyses." Together with language and mathematics, this linear construction of temporal experience constitutes the essence of the active Western mode of consciousness.

The present is understood as precariously binding past and future together: the moment we try to pin it down, it is either a "no more" or a "not yet," as Hannah Arendt has noted:

> From that perspective, the enduring present looks like an extended "now"—a contradiction in terms—as though the thinking ego were capable of stretching the moment out and

thus producing a kind of spatial habitat for itself. But this seeming spatiality of a temporal phenomenon is an error, caused by the metaphors we traditionally use in terminology dealing with the phenomenon of Time. As Bergson first discovered, they are all terms "borrowed from spatial language. . . . If we want to reflect on time, it is space that responds." Thus "duration is always expressed as extension," and the past is understood as something lying [physically] *behind* us, the future as lying somewhere *ahead* of us.

In these ways, Western precepts of time are not only material in terms of the so-called organs that serve as "biological clocks" or the mechanisms of actual time-keeping, but it is also made implacably material by our language-bound confusion of time as a spatially and physically constructed phenomenon.

Primal consciousness is larger than the psychological geography by which the West knows it. It overflows linearity in dreams, imaginings, visions, intuitions, and all those quintessential and amorphous experiences that must call upon metaphor in order to surface into Western mentality. Alternative modes of consciousness, like meditation, seek to undo the dogma of linearity. Many hallucinogenic drugs overwhelm the linear perspective and induce experiences outside the confines of clock-time. But it is doubtlessly in the arts of the West that we discover the most luminous excursions into alternative modes of time. And of these arts, literature is the most duplex, chasing after both "realities" and "shadows" with equal vigor. T. S. Eliot's distinction between Shakespeare's and Dante's uses of simile provides the two dominant modes of literary imagination in the West: "Whereas the simile of Dante is merely to make you see how the people looked, and is explanatory, the figure of Shakespeare is expansive rather than intensive; its purpose is to *add* to what you see."

Scientists, like Dante, build explanations and describe appearances; visionaries like Shakespeare attempt to expand what we experience. These two constructs that epitomize Western dualism are, among primal peoples, a continuum so elaborate, as we shall see in discussing the mentality of the Hopi Indians of the American Southwest, that it fundamentally shapes their language into grammatical forms totally remote from the syntax of European languages.

The visionary images of recent Western literature, like the syntax of primal people such as the Hopi, provide a nonlinear perspective alien in the West ever since the rise of Aristotelian realism. It is a vantage as urgently needed in science as it is in art. As Robert Ornstein has pointed out: "That we now lack a psychological framework for these nonlinear time experiences means not that they should be ignored entirely, but that we must develop a suitable structure if we are to incorporate them into contemporary science."

NOTES ON THE RESTORATION
OF A VISIONARY LITERATURE

Literary critic Lionel Trilling was outspoken in his classic book *The Liberal Imagination;* the present direction of literature, he believed, is utterly disastrous. The so-called "poetic methods being employed by some contemporary novelists mark the end of an ending." What we really need to do, according to Trilling, is to rediscover the art of "storytelling." We must get back to "natural prose" and "good common speech." We are told that "a prose which approaches poetry has no doubt its own value, but it cannot serve to repair the loss of a straightforward prose, rapid, masculine, and committed to events, making its effects not by the single word or by the phrase but by words properly and naturally massed." Clearly Lionel Trilling was a spokesman for the revival of a faltering naturalism. Most of the really important writers of the last half of the twentieth century ignored his mandate.

"Quite a few protests have been aired in recent years against the sway of the naturalist method in fiction," Philip Rahv wrote in his landmark essay "Notes on the Decline of Naturalism." "It is charged that this method treats material in a manner so flat and external as to inhibit the search for value and meaning, and that in any case it is now exhausted." The kind of writing that Trilling favored and Rahv disdained is (an endless bookkeeping of existence.) Such ledgered "objectivity" is not possible in a society in which there is no central and sustaining value system, with accessible and significant symbols and forms. Such realistic books can only be written for readers who have not yet emerged into the contemporary predicament and are continuing to live in an ideological past. They do not realize that life is nowhere seen steadily and whole, but under a number of perspectives relative to nothing central. Never has the interpretation of cultures been so worldwide, or disintegration so universal.

Behind all literature is a common expressive impulse. But expressiveness is not a single, uniform power in any art. It constantly changes, at least on a certain level, as public values change. What is amusing to one era is not necessarily amusing to another. What is tragic in one age is not necessarily tragic in another. The quality of sentience changes from one era to the next, and in ways so subtle that even the most undefinable qualities of life—those with no direct relationship to emotion—also change.

The kind of straightforward storytelling demanded by Lionel Trilling is wishful thinking in our era. It cannot exist without faith, and faith in the West is obsolescent. Western literature, with its clock-time and geographical space, faces the same problems of credibility faced by organized religion.

The alternative to the bankruptcy of literary naturalism has preoccupied many of the most celebrated critics and writers of the West. "The literature of vision," as David Daiches calls this alternative form, "tends to come into prose as a part of the reaction against what is regarded as an over-formulated, and therefore not sufficiently objective, type of fable literature." The personal sense of truth replaces the formulas of a civilization. The paradox found here is a search for objectivity leading to greater subjectivity.

This "literature of vision," as Daiches called it, is very different from prior literary forms dominant in the West. First of all, the subject matter is not fitted into a linear structure and organized on the basis of character motivation and the succession of events. Kenneth Burke distinguishes two kinds of literary composition: "syllogistic progression," in which the reader is led from one part of the composition to another by means of logical relationships; and "qualitative progression," in which the reader is led, according to a "logic of feeling," by means of association and contrast. What Burke has called qualitative progression is the core of visionary literature—the expressive mode of the dreamtime so familiar to primal peoples.

"Like all the other symbolic forms, art is not the mere reproduction of a ready-made and given reality. It is one of the ways leading to an objective view of things and of human life. It is not an imitation but a *discovery* of reality. We do not, however, discover nature through art in the same sense in which the scientist uses the term 'nature.'... When the scientist describes an object he characterizes it by a set of numbers, by its physical and chemical constants. Art has not only a different aim but a different object." (Ernst Cassirer, *An Essay on Man*)

Supporting these refutations of naturalism are mostly those writers who look to symbolism, fantasy, and myth. "The younger writers," Rahv wrote in 1949, "are stirred by the ambition to create a new type of imaginative prose into which the recognizably real enters as one component rather than as the total substance. They want to break the novel of its objective habits; some want to introduce into it philosophical ideas; others are not so much drawn to expressing ideas as to expressing the motley strivings of the inner self—dreams, visions, and fantasies."

These writers have steadily produced a new "popular" fiction since 1945—attracting the massive population of the college-trained and radically changed Baby Boom generation while having minimal impact on the mass market of literature. They have made fundamental alterations in the way Western readers normally "performed a book," to use Vonnegut's metaphor, and their books tend to verge on the cinematic. "Events," Harry Levin commented in his discussion of James Joyce in 1941, "are reported when and as they occur; the tense is a continuous present." That description is close to the dreamtime—temporal consciousness—of primal peoples. "In its intimacy and in its continuity," Levin continues, "*Ulysses* has more in common with the cinema than with other fiction. The movement of Joyce's style, the thought of his characters, is like unreeling film; his method of construction, the arrangement of this raw material, involves the crucial operation of *montage*."

This kind of vision of time and space bears the same relation to ordinary Western fiction that the film does to the stage. The time and space of the cinema are essentially abstract. In the early days of film-making it was traditional to hire great actors of the stage, like Sarah Bernhardt, and to film silent sequences of classic melodramas with the stationary camera focused on the entire stage from the vantage of a spectator in the third row. There were no close-ups, none of the exceptional intimacy of the later cinema, no movement of the camera, no flashbacks or any other manipulations of time. Event followed event in strict clock-time, producing an internal rhythm which, as we view most of these old films today, seems painfully tedious and slow. Nothing better illustrates the naturalistic bookkeeping of existence.

It was only gradually that the temporal and spatial attitudes of cinema (and literature) fundamentally altered the Western traditions of perception. "It is no more true to say of Joyce, than any other artist," Levin concludes, "that his work enlarges the domain of consciousness. . . . Bergson himself, the philosopher who held the fullest realization of the fluid nature of time and experience, also held that the intellect 'spatializes.' Consequently our imitations of life, no matter how complete and complicated we try to make them, are bound to be one-sided and over-simple." The intellect spatializes—and only in the dreamtime of primal peoples and poets and dreamers can we fully grasp the ineffable that lingers just beyond the reach of intelligence.

There were other long-range factors that made for the decline of naturalism. Through the influence of psychology Western literature recovered its inwardness, which combines the naturalistic description of the mental process with the antinaturalistic depiction of the subjective and irrational. Another factor is the tendency of naturalism, as Thomas Mann observed in his remarks on Zola, to turn into the mythic through sheer immersion in the typical. It seems apparent that naturalism cannot hope to survive the world of nineteenth-century science and industry of which it was the product. For what is the crisis of reality in contemporary art and society if not at bottom the crisis of the dissolution of this familiar world? Naturalism, which exhausted itself in taking an inventory of this world while it was still relatively stable, cannot possibly do justice to the phenomena of its own decline.

A new visionary literature has gradually come into existence. This radical alteration in Western viewpoint has not simply affected the subject matter of writing but has, more essentially, produced an entirely new technique for dealing with time, space, and character.

As we have suspected since the time of Shelley and as we have decisively known since Walt Whitman, poetry has largely abandoned the expository mood of Dante, Pope, and Dryden. It has assumed in the West so metaphoric an attitude that we commonly use the term "poetic" as an opposite of "realistic." The Spanish poet Federico García Lorca was profoundly aware of both the amorphous potential of imagery and the visionary mentality of Spanish gypsies which he used to support his luminous metaphors:

> August,
> counterpoints
> of sugar and peach,
> and the sun with the afternoon
> like a fruit's core.
> The ear of grain keeps intact
> its hard yellow laughter.
> August.
> Children eat
> brown bread and delicious moon.   (E. HONIG)

But visionary mentality is not limited in the West to poetry and so-called poetic license. From Tolstoy's fearsome image of "a peasant muttering something . . . working at the iron," which haunts Anna Karenina, to the famous apparition of wild horses which appears to Gerald in D. H. Lawrence's *Women in Love*, an alternative, "cinematic" abstraction of time and space has come to dominate the most notable writing of the twentieth century.

Meanwhile those who are reactionary or faithful or both continue to require discursive explanations, like the scholarly editor who once asked me exactly what period of history I was referring to in the phrase: "The dwellers of caves in the early morning of this human world built scaffolds in the dark interiors of their rock caverns." I tried to explain that precise information would not enhance what I was attempting to say, but that the "early morning of this human world" might support an important feeling. A date would only convince the reader that he had understood my point when, in fact, he would have missed it utterly if all he came away with was a historical incident. In this way, in literature and in the mentality of primal peoples there is a visionary facility that imparts a separate reality—a form of communication with an alternative objective. This alternative is not a beautified phrase or an illusive verbal dodge; it is not a substitution for "straightforward prose, rapid, masculine, and committed to events." It is an effort, contrarily, to get the "language" out of literature by refusing to accept the traditional responsibility of writers to depict "realistically" what is before them and what is happening to them.

All of us know that there is an enormous, inexpressible gap between what we feel and the words at our command for depicting our experiences. This situation is especially apparent if we are writers—the sort of craftspeople who use words for more than matter-of-fact daily existence. The results of this predicament are far too complicated for me to discuss here, but some of them are relevant to the methods of visionary literature generally, and especially to the way the primal mind deals with time.

The more we are confronted as writers with the nearly unbearable materiality of words, the more we grasp that the very syntax of language which allows us to communicate also automatically limits and defines what we are able to say in a given language. Some writers react to this conclusiveness of Western words by becoming intrigued by the process of writing as a thing unto itself. They look for shortcuts that could lead directly from what is felt to the page itself. For this reason, many of the works of visionary literature are emblematic forms built out of the medium of writing without the intrusion of the process by which language normally communicates and therefore shapes and limits the so-called bounds of Western literature.

We see a good many Western writers who are producing new forms by ridiculing the methodologies of older literary

idioms. Some of these pieces are fairly straightforward paro-
dies; some take their lead from the Imagists of 1909–17 or the
Dadaists of a later decade—concerned primarily with the
shape the writing takes on the printed pages itself. But perhaps the most interesting visionary pieces are those depart-
ing entirely from the conventional notion of "filling the
page with ideas in the form of language" and creating a literature that views the very space of the page (its surfaces,
edges, etc.) and the very duration needed to see or to read
the page as an emblematic theatre where time, motion, image, succession, and forms have lives of their own.

What visionary literature makes clear is that many writers
of the West have asserted new ideas of what writing is all
about, and in doing this they have produced effects with
words, pages, ink, typewriters, found materials, and print
which imply an entirely original method of turning experience into pages. Curiously, this "new" approach strongly resembles American Indian Rock Art—that ancient blending
of graphics, poetry, and ritual which spoke of *art* before
there was a word for it.

TIME IN THE WORLD OF HOPI INDIANS

"Hopi language," wrote Benjamin Lee Whorf in his landmark essay "An American Indian Model of the Universe,"
"is seen to contain no words, grammatical forms, construc-
tions or expressions that refer directly to what we call 'time,'
or to past, present, or future, or to enduring or lasting, or to
motion as kinematic rather than dynamic. . . . Hence, the
Hopi language contained no reference to 'time,' either explicit or implicit."

Though Native American mentality is not uniform and
though there are roughly two hundred distinctly different
Indian languages (some as remote from one another as Chinese is from English) spoken in North America alone, we

can effectively trace a pervasive aspect of a metaphysics that permeates the cultural character of most, if not all, Native American tribes of North America. The language of the Hopi (living in Arizona) is especially revealing in terms of the way language conceptualizes our understanding of that experience called "time" and then automatically structures that concept into oral and written literary traditions.

Whorf observes: "Just as it is possible to have any number of geometries other than the Euclidean which gives an equally perfect account of space configurations, so it is possible to have descriptions of the universe, all equally valid, that do not contain our familiar contrasts of time and space." In this manner the Hopi language and culture betray a different metaphysics from the West.

In the Hopi view, the element of time disappears utterly— at least as the West knows it*—and space is fundamentally altered as a conception, so that it is no longer the homogeneous and instantaneous timeless space of our supposed intuition or of classical Newtonian mechanics. This process of conceptualization, however, is not minimal or crude by any means. New concepts and abstractions flow into the Hopi worldview, describing the cosmos without reference to Western time or space. These Hopi abstractions usually appear to the Western mind as rather mystical or, at least, highly psychological in character, for they do not easily fit into the sensibility or languages of the dominant societies. "They are ideas," Whorf states, "which we are accustomed to consider as part and parcel either of so-called animistic or vitalistic beliefs, or of those transcendental unifications of experience and intuitions of things unseen that are felt by the

---

*In Hopi, like most Indian languages, temporal thinking is so drastically different from the ideas of Western time that there are no divisions such as hours, minutes, seconds, etc.—and the only designations of time are related to the experience of night and day, the phases of the moon, and the solstices, etc. The Blackfeet count "years" by summers and divide time into two annual seasons.

consciousness of the mystic, or which are given out in mystical and so-called occult systems of thought." But these precepts which might appear exotic and perhaps absurd to the Western mind are given explicit form in the Hopi language and are implicit in its very structure and grammar. Whorf continues:

> If mystical be perchance a term of abuse in the eyes of a modern Western scientist, it must be emphasized that these underlying abstractions and postulates of the Hopian metaphysics are, from a detached viewpoint, equally (or to the Hopi, more) justified pragmatically and experientially, as compared to the flowing time and static space of our own metaphysics, which are *au fond* equally mystical. The metaphysics underlying our own language, thinking, and modern culture (I speak not of the recent and quite different relativity metaphysics of modern science) imposes upon the universe two grand cosmic forms, space and time; static three-dimensional infinite space, and kinetic one-dimensional uniformly and perpetually flowing time—two utterly separate and unconnected aspects of reality according to this familiar way of thinking. The [Western] flow of time is, in turn, the subject of a threefold division: past, present, and future.

This is not to say that the Hopi metaphysics does not also possess cosmic forms comparable to—though distinctly different from—the Western notions of scale and scope; but it operates far more the way contemporary artists function as "aliens" within the dominant society—people who are peculiarly and marvelously devoted to the evolution of a metaphysics called "art." Categorical thinking means very little to most artists; they are concerned with a more holistic vision which they strive to bring into a culture whose language makes no allowances for anything but the categorical. Contrarily, for the Hopi the aesthetic is intrinsic to daily life and viewpoint; so there is no gap between what is experienced and what is expressed.

> The objective or manifested comprises all that is or has been accessible to the senses, the historical physical universe, in fact, with no attempt to distinuguish between present and past, but excluding everything that we call future, but not merely this; it includes equally and indistinguishably all that we call mental—everything that appears or exists in the mind, or, as the Hopi would prefer to say, in the heart, not only the heart of man, but the heart of animals, plants, and things, and behind and within all the forms and appearances of nature in the heart of nature.

This linguistic observation by Whorf reaffirms the description of anthropologist Paul Radin, who explained back in the 1930s that Indians do not share the white man's inclination to separate experience into the linear realms of objective and subjective mentality; that Indians include in their grasp of reality everything that is felt, experienced, dreamed about, envisioned, hoped for, etc. Yet this is not to suggest a uniformity that disregards the contrasting aspects of consciousness; for the Hopi also envision a subjective frame of mind (subjective, as Whorf points out, only from the Western viewpoint, since for the Hopi it is "intensely real and quivering with life, power, and potency"). This temporal idea embraces not only the Western concept of "future" but also all mentality, intellection, and emotion. This is the realm of expectancy, of desire and purpose, of vitalizing processes—inspiration—"the realm of thought thinking itself out from an inner realm (the Hopi heart) into manifestation."

The subjective side of Hopi thinking is difficult for the Western person to understand and is best described as "that which is beginning to emerge into manifestation . . . beginning to be done . . . but is not yet in full operation." These indirect depictions of a formative process are essential, since in the Hopi language there are no verbs corresponding to the English "come" or "go" that mean simple and abstract motion of a purely kinematic way of thinking. Hopi terms for "to come" tend to mean "eventuates to here," "eventuate from it," "arrived," etc. "Thus," Whorf concludes, "this nearer edge of the subjective cuts across and includes a part of our [Western] present time, viz. the moment of inception, but most of our present belongs in the scheme to the objective realm and so is indistinguishable from our past."

To the Hopi there is no temporal future; there is nothing in the subjective state corresponding to the sequences and successions conjoined with distances and changing physical configurations that the West finds in the objective world. The Hopi conceive time and motion in the objective realm in a purely operational sense—constantly turning the Western notions about *things* into propositions about *events*.

As we shall see, Native American literature is deeply touched by this distinctive grasp of a subjective/objective relationship in the cosmos. "There comes a point," Whorf concludes in his landmark essay, "where extension in detail ceases to be knowable and is lost in the vast distance, and where the subjective, creeping behind the scenes as it were, merges into the objective, so that at this inconceivable distance from the observer—from all observers—there is an all-encircling end and beginning of things where it might be said that existence itself swallows up the objective and the subjective."

This concept is the black hole as history . . . the event horizon and the abysm of antiquity. It is the time and place told about in the myths, which are known only subjectively or mentally. The Hopi realize and even express in their grammar that the things recalled in myths do not have the same kind of reality as things of the present day, the things of practical concern. The dim past of myths is thus reached subjectively through the vertical axis of reality. Hence that realm is placed below the present surface of the earth, though this does not mean that the land of the Hopi origin myths is a hole or cavern as we tend to understand it. It is *Palátkwapi*, a land like our present earth, but to which our earth bears the relation of a distant sky. That sky is pierced by the heroes of myths who transcend the objective and subjective and provide Indians with the worldview of their literature.*

THE TEMPORAL MENTALITY OF NATIVE AMERICAN LITERATURE

There are three fundamental forms of American Indian literature. There is the one largely invented by Charles Eastman and, later, by D'Arcy McNickle—an Indianized realism which, as Oliver La Farge once said, was "simple, direct, devoid of affectations, and fast-moving."

As much as I admire *Indian Boyhood* by Eastman and *The Surrounded* by McNickle, theirs is not the kind of Indian literary mentality I hope to discuss here, but rather a very traditional Western approach to experience which Indians adopted to their purpose of writing about Indian Life.

There are a number of writers whose works fall into this general kind of Western *realism:* with apparent influences from sociopolitical writers like Steinbeck and Dos Passos, with stylistic influences from Faulkner and Hemingway. The excellent stories of Simon J. Ortiz (Acoma Pueblo) fit into this frame of mind; so do the novels of the distinguished Blackfeet writer James Welch. There are also elements in the writing of the 1969 Pulitzer Prize–winning Kiowa Indian author, N. Scott Momaday, which borrow

---

*An important elaboration of some of these ideas is found in La Barre's *The Human Animal*, pp. 197–198.

heavily from the realism of Western literature. But in Moma-day's writings there are two other, very influential elements. He has brilliantly dealt with a kind of "holy tradition" in his books—a style aimed at conveying the core of Indian cere-monialism. He has also anticipated a kind of visionary writ-ing that finds its contemporary epitome in the prose of Craig Kee Strete and Leslie Marmon Silko and in most Indian po-etry, but especially in the poems of Roberta Hill, Joseph Bru-chac, Duane Niatum, Leslie Silko, James Welch, and Ray A. Young Bear.

Probably the most controversial Indian writer concerned with "holy tradition" is Hyemeyohsts Storm. Like N. Scott Momaday before him, Storm is essentially concerned with the kind of arduous communication that Carlos Castaneda has attempted so brilliantly—the transliteration from one culture to another of central metaphysical ideas. It is a litera-ture requiring a capacity to create parables and imagery born of poetry; but it is not truly poetic so much as it is expository and didactic. It has as its primary purpose the instruction of readers in the mentality of Indian tradition, and though the viewpoint is totally immersed in the tradition being de-scribed, the writing is *about* that tradition and is not an ex-tension of that tradition into a distinctive literary form.

The fictional writings of Leslie Silko and Craig Kee Strete represent a force in Indian literature somewhat similar to the efforts of Indian painters in the 1960s to break away from the Traditional style of painting and to produce an idiosyn-cratic idiom—an unapologetic extension of tribal mentality into a new and innovative personal form. There is no ques-tion whatever of Silko's success in writing directly *out of* her Laguna Pueblo tradition, rather than simply writing *about* it. Even in her realistic short stories where the focus is on unso-phisticated people, there is always an intimation of a reality larger and essentially different from that of the dominant so-ciety and its predominantly naturalistic literature. And in her novel of 1977, *Ceremony*, Silko makes no effort to disguise the fact that she is attempting in style, structure, point of view, temporal and spatial depictions, to create a new Indian literature.

Craig Kee Strete works in a somewhat different manner, but the end result is very similar to the effect of Silko's *Ceremony*. Committed to professional writing and therefore automatically committed to realism, Kee Strete invokes "science fiction" as a means of describing the metaphysics of Indian mentality which, in the realist mentality, automatically turn into fantasy. His collection of stories, *The Bleeding Man and Other Science Fiction Stories*, contains uncommonly fine pieces; while his novel of 1978, *Paint Your Face on a Drowning in the River*, nearly achieves the refinement, mysteriousness, and expressiveness of Silko's *Ceremony*.

It is only in this new, visionary Indian literature that we discover the rebirth of the ancient ritualism of the oral tradition (I speak now of the noninstructional and therefore nonexpository aspects of the oral tradition). Much as Joyce produced an "Irish" literature out of the European naturalistic novel, much as García Lorca created a visionary folk style out of the formalism of the Andalusian poet of the Renaissance, Luis de Gongora, so Silko constructed a ritualized fiction that truly bends the connotation of the term "novel."

Ceremony is about Tayo, an American Indian veteran of World War II who returns home in a state of exhaustion, depression, and shock. In the South Pacific he watched his half-brother die. He also saw the execution of many Japanese prisoners of war who, to Tayo, looked very much like his own brother and gradually came to represent a "hated" Asian population not unlike the Indians at home. Silko does not simply make this emotional and haunting global analogy in discursive language, she also develops a strong metaphor connecting the atom bomb dropped on Hiroshima with the first tests of that weapon in New Mexico, near Los

Alamos, on the very land taken from the Indian people of the Pueblo of Cochiti.

The focus of the novel is on Tayo's search for the sanity he lost in the white man's war. He goes to Gallup, that tough and racist little town near the Arizona border where tourists flock to see "real Indians." There Tayo encounters Old Betonie, a man who knows Indian curative medicine and who therefore attempts to exorcise the evil of Tayo's military experiences. The central ceremony involves the use of sandpainting and prayer sticks—a healing ritual very ancient in the Southwest of America.

As Frank MacShane wrote in *The New York Times Book Review* (June 12, 1977):

> Leslie Silko's method of narration imitates the ceremony itself, *for she shifts her story from one time and place to another until eventually everything is made clear.* These shifts are not disruptive, however, for the story is always vivid and concrete. When Tayo stands on the bridge overlooking the shacks along the river bank where the prostitutes live, it is evident that he was once there as a child, himself the product of some hasty union, hiding furtively while his mother met a customer. The novel is full of dramatic encounters, barroom fights, drunken drives in pick-up trucks across the barren countryside, ugly meetings with white landowners. [Silko's] achievement lies partly in the way she has woven together the European tradition of the novel with American Indian story-telling. She has used animal stories and legends to give a fabulous dimension to her novel. These are set aside from the prose narrative and look like curative and ceremonial chants that are recited in hogans (the Navajo traditional home). All of these devices reflect the theme of the novel, which is that the war has made all people one, "united by a circle of death that devoured people in cities twelve thousand miles away, victims who had never known these mesas, who had never seen the delicate colors of the rocks which boiled up their slaughter."

Among the Indians of the Americas the tellers of stories
are weavers, the makers of *cultural autobiographies.* Their designs are the threads of their personal sagas as well as the
history of their whole people. Though the designs are always traditional, the hands that weave them are always
new. These Indian stories, like ancient designs in textiles and
pottery, have been passed from one generation to the next
and sometimes they were written down by ethnologists and
by priests who had a curiously contradictory interest in the
cultures they were anxious to eradicate.

In the oral tradition, like so-called Traditional Indian
painting, the expression of the "individual" was important
but not primary. The pre-Columbian tribes were so homogeneous as to make elaborate scene-setting, character descriptions, etc. not only unnecessary—for almost everyone knew
the stories well but took great pleasure in their repetition—
but undesirable as unsubtle and prosaic, qualities not much
admired by Indians who are generally a most poetic people.
But the art of storytelling, like the art of painting, has
changed a great deal for Indians in the last two decades.
There has been a disinclination to stick with the Western
conception of style and with the white man's precepts of reality. Like modern Indian painters, young Indian writers
have made use of new potentials of technique and imagination learned through the education available in the twentieth century—both in the Indian traditions and in the
cultures of the dominant societies.

These visionary writers believe, as do contemporary Indian painters, in the existence of some sort of transcendent Indian sensibility, and they believe that its power and its truth
can be expressed in modes typical of our day as well as in
the venerated, unique styles of the older traditionalists. Just
as young Indian painters with a command of modern methods and a personal style have reinterpreted Indian iconography and history in new ways which finally touch upon a

substance of Indian vision, so writers have attempted to recount folk history and contemporary Indian predicaments in a prose that tries to merge the old and the new, the essential poetry of Indian viewpoint with the fundamental realism of Western mentality.

In writing a novel about the end of the Aztec domain from the native viewpoint, I discovered a number of valuable records that preserved the Aztec descriptions of the invasion. I think it might be of interest to trace various versions of the stories I recounted in *The Sun, He Dies*, since they provide a very credible example of how multifaceted reality is, depending on whose point of view you are seeing.

In one example, the description of the first time any of the Aztecs experienced the burst of guns or cannons, we find five exceptionally disparate versions of seemingly "the same event." I have reprinted five versions of this event—since the various texts are short and perfectly demonstrate the kind of language that results when several different writers from highly different cultures approached the same sixteenth-century event.

In the various tellings of the story of the "first burst of the cannons," all the writers (and translators) intend to report the same event and all of the accounts are intended to be history. But what we find when we read these versions are five strikingly different "visions" and not the objective reporting which we are led to believe is the true basis of *objective history*. Between these vastly different versions there exists not misjudgment, not exaggeration or fraud, but a real and fundamental variance in the way different people experience reality: time, space, succession, characters, etc. No wonder, then, the need for an Indian literature that does not lean on Western preconceptions but evolves styles and structures capable of supporting the distinctive Indian metaphysics. The version transcribed from reports of Aztec survivors, c. 1547, by Fray Bernardino de Sahagun in the language of the Aztec, Nahuatl:

Niman tlanaoati in capitan injc ilpiloque, tepoztli imjcxic qujntlalilique, yoan inquechtlan: in ie iuhquj njman ic qujtlazque in tomaoac tleqjqujztli: auh in titlanti in jquac in vel iolmjcque, yoan cocotlaoaque, vehuetzque, nenecujliuhtivetzque, aocmo qujmatque: auh in espanoles qujmeeuhq qujmeeoatitlalique, qujmonjitique vino: njma ie ic qujntlamaca, qujntlaqualtique, ic imjhio qujcujque, ic oalihiocujque.

The translation from the Aztec into English by Arthur J. O. Anderson and Charles E. Dibble:

> Then the Captain commanded that they be bound. They put irons on their ankles and their necks. This done, they then shot the great lombard gun. And the messengers, when this [happened], indeed fainted away and swooned; they each fell: each one, swaying, fell; they knew no more. And the Spaniards raised each one, raised each one so that he sat; they made them drink wine. Thereupon they gave them food; they made them eat. Thus they restored them; thus they retained their strength.

The version translated from Nahuatl into Spanish by Angel Maria Garibay K, recreated in Spanish by Miguel Leon-Portilla, and rendered in English by Lysander Kemp:

> Then the Captain gave orders, and the messengers were chained by the feet and by the neck. When this had been done, the great cannon was fired off. The messengers lost their senses and fainted away. They fell down side by side and lay where they had fallen. But the Spaniards quickly revived them: they lifted them up, gave them wine to drink and then offered them food.

The version of the same event as recounted by the famous soldier of Fernando Cortes's invasion forces, Bernal Díaz, in his memoir entitled *The Conquest of New Spain* (this translation by J. M. Cohen):

> The display was carried out in the presence of the two ambassadors [of Montezuma], and in order that they should see the shot leave the gun Cortes pretended that he wished to

speak to them and some other Caciques again, just before the cannon was fired. As it was very still at that moment, the balls resounded with a great din as they went over the forest. The two governors and the rest of the Indians were frightened by this strange happening, and ordered their painters to paint it, so that Montezuma might see.

The same event as reported by William H. Prescott in his famous *The Conquest of Mexico:*

[Cortes] ordered out the cavalry on the beach, the wet sands of which afforded a firm footing for the horses. The bold and rapid movements of the troops, as they went through their military exercises; the apparent ease with which they managed the fiery animals on which they were mounted; the glancing of their weapons; and the shrill cry of the trumpet, all filled the spectators with astonishment but when they heard the thunders of the cannon, which Cortes ordered to be fired at the same time, and witnessed the volumes of smoke and flame issuing from these terrible engines, and the rushing sound of the balls, as they dashed through the trees of the neighboring forest, shivering their branches into fragments, they were filled with consternation, from which the Aztec chief himself was not wholly free.

Unquestionably in matters of fact and, alas, in terms of humanity, the victors and the victims saw the same events very differently—to such an extent that more than three hundred years after the Spanish reports of the invasion, Prescott (who was essentially very fair-minded) nonetheless sustained the bias of the victors even though he possessed all the conflicting accounts of the Aztecs themselves in the works of Sahagun, Duran, etc. To the Indian "writers" the ambassadors of Montezuma were chained and brutalized; while to the non-Indian writers the messengers of Montezuma were simply given a harmless demonstration of military might. Of course both versions are intended as correct, but we do not really comprehend what happened unless we are in possession of the various responses to the same event. There is no "truth" to be found here. What is discovered in history is a cultural viewpoint.

Besides the variance in our experience of history there is also a variance in the way we experience ourselves. The conception of "characterization" in Western literature and the literature of primal cultures is sometimes at odds. Primal people and the people of the dominant cultures tend to understand themselves as persons in quite different ways. Pre-Columbian literature is tribal rather than individuated. But this tribalism is not limited to American Indians or the peoples of Oceania and Africa; it is also found in various European traditions, like that of Homer. The "characterizations" in both the European sagas and those of Native Americans are similar in many ways, and they are fundamentally different from later notions of personality in literary works. The dramatis personae of tribal literature are essentially external. The reader tends to know characters by their actions and not by an outpouring of feelings and various internal states of mind. To the cursory view such characters might seem to be stereotypes, but on the long view they are actually archetypes. To the primal mind truth is not inclusive but essential. In folk literature the "truth" is made up of what lies at the bottom of various events of a perpetual now, while to the Western mind the "truth" is *everything* that makes up a chronological succession of events.

Gradually, however, a change comes over traditional folk literature. In post-Columbian times the attitude toward character changes markedly without ever relinquishing its primal focus. Literary characters tend to be individuated in much the same way that Native American painters, who once depicted tribal "beings" rather than "individuals," begin to represent specific persons in their paintings. This "Shakespearean" perspective of human psychology is not necessarily the result of Western influences, but probably evolves from the pressures and cultural shock of confrontation between radically different peoples. Whatever the cause, the result is substantially Indian. The archetypes have become diversified and evasive, but they are never caricatures of ideas and persons. They never turn into allegorical figures, but remain characters in the Homeric sense. Unlike Studs Lonigan or Stephen Dedalus, who are individuals in terms of the Western view of personality, the characters of Indian and other primal literatures are Platonic models rather than psychological case histories. For primal peoples tend to strive for the depiction of essences rather than appearances.

In *The Magic Mountain*, Thomas Mann saw this visionary perspective as a projection into consciousness of the Jungian dreamtime: "Now I know that it is not out of our single souls we dream. We dream anonymously and communally, if each after his fashion. The great soul of which we are a part may dream through us, in our manner of dreaming, its own secret dreams, of its youth, its hope, its joy and peace—and its blood-sacrifice."

That mordant dream, that repertory of primal myths and visions of the dreamtime, conceals itself among the corridors where realism cannot find its way. The events of the Indian cosmos, as Joseph Epes Brown explained, are understood neither in terms of time past nor time future. "They speak rather to a perennial reality of the now." It is this temporal revelation which lies at the farthest alcove of the Indian visionary's mind; it is this immediacy which proclaims the preciousness of the instant, the ever-changing, ever-modulating Indian moment that is a perpetual *Now*.

5

PLACE

Jackson Pollock tried to get through and beyond the restrictions of physical reality and to capture and transmit a distillation of energy, drawn out of the flux of human experience and thrown back again into the flux of time.
—BRYAN ROBERTSON

Our sense of place—of space—is largely determined by the manner in which we see ourselves in relation to nature. Perspective is the art of delineating solid objects upon a plane surface so as to produce the same conception of relative positions and magnitudes, or of distance, as we conceptualize out of our cultural experience of space in nature. Perspective is the result of how we interpret and therefore see space. It is a highly ethnocentric interpretation existing in numerous forms, but the most characteristic ones are these. *Tiered Perspective:* suggesting space by placing levels of activity one above another, the lowest level in the composition reading as the frontal plane. *Isometric Perspective:* parallel lines do not converge, objects do not get smaller as they recede, but depth is suggested by providing two points of view and using the flatness of the painted surface as an aesthetic entity. *Aerial Perspective:* since air is not entirely transparent, an ever-increasing layer of obscuring atmosphere gradually interpolates itself between the seen objects and the viewer; therefore as objects get smaller with distance, the eye fails to see detail and contrasts diminish as they turn to a middle gray. *Linear Perspective:* suggests space by the use of the mathematical conception of the oblique line—parallel lines (edges of planes) *appear* to converge as they become more distant from the observer, and if uninterrupted they converge at a point on the horizon line (actual curvature of the earth and the viewer's eye level), and the objects close to the observer overlay and obscure more distant objects when they are in the same trajectory of vision.

POLLOCK AND THE NAVAJOS

Linear Perspective is, of course, the predominant Western way of seeing. Painting, however, since the end of the nineteenth century has rebelliously countered all "rules" governing the depiction of space, generally, and the use of formal perspective, specifically. Picasso, inspired by African masks, helped to develop Cubism, while the American abstract expressionist Jackson Pollock, inspired by Navajo sandpainting, rejected Cubism and developed action and field painting. As Alberto Busignani noted: "Pollock released art in the United States from its long European bondage" and reinvented a vision of space and place that is distinctly Indian in its mentality.

Gary Witherspoon has written with great perception about the relationship of Pollock's innovative art to the primal minds of Navajo sandpainters and ceremonialists. He indicates that "Navajo art has had a subtle, little-known relationship with and impact upon contemporary art." Pollock was born in Wyoming and spent his youth in the Southwest where he often visited Indian settlements. "My painting does not come from the easel," Pollock once explained. "I hardly ever stretch my canvas before painting. I prefer to tack the unstretched canvas to the hard wall or floor, I need the resistance of a hard surface. On the floor I am at ease. I feel nearer, more a part of the painting, since this way I can walk around it, work from the four sides and literally be 'in' the painting. This is akin to the method of the Indian sand-painters of the West."

Pollock rejected the Western limits placed on the experience of space. He also rejected most of the technological elements of Western society. He claimed that the orientation toward production and consumption of things reduced humanity and the natural environment to mere episodes of the productive machine. In his 1971 book *Pollock,* critic Alberto Busignani stated that Pollock's dismissal of the traditions of his culture was "accompanied by his acceptance of another kind of history, intimately linked to nature, magic, symbols, etc. . . . Pollock found it recorded in the practices of the American Indians, especially in the sandpaintings of the Navajo."

The metaphysics underlying Pollock's art is far more than a matter of appearances or avant-garde rebelliousness. His pictorial effort was to unify the picture by unifying experience and by seeing all things in the cosmos as part of a vast general order. He sought to avoid fragmentation for its own sake or for the sake of decoration.

Pollock was not simply dealing with decorative abstraction; his purpose was far more complex, which may help to explain how he became the catalyst for the most heterogeneous and persuasive movement in American art, Abstract Expressionism.

As Busignani stated in his appraisal of Pollock, he achieved "a conception of existence which brought together history and nature, past, present and future in the act of creation." For him "the only morality, and therefore the only truth, lies in becoming totally intermingled with one's creation, making painting and the act of painting a constant intervention into reality." Pollock's art, and therefore Navajo Indian art as well, was a seminal force in the evolution of color field painting—the dominant art and most significant style of the past few decades.

The art of Jackson Pollock and of Native Americans mandates the integration of history and nature in the act of creation; this art revives the organic relationship between painterly space and the sacredness of *place*. It replaces the intrusion of mathematics upon the way in which we see and know space with an alternative realization of space as the embodiment of events and beings and powers. As Joseph Epes Brown has noted, "Native experiences of place are infused with mythic themes. These express events of sacred time, which are as real now as in any time. They are experienced through each landmark of each people's immediate natural environment, . . . thus, it gives meaning to the life of man who cannot conceive of himself apart from the land."

SACRED SPACE

Though Indian art demonstrates the way in which primal mentality constructs a manifestation of *place* out of the ideal of space, it is in Indian architecture that we best witness the intrinsic amalgamation of space and place, of place and nature, of man and nature. Not only Native Americans but all primal peoples have always found the means by which to be protected from the infinity of space. The tipi, the hogan, or the longhouse, just as the temple, cathedral, or the ceremonial center of antiquity, determines the perimeters of space in such a way that a sacred place is established. The defined space—the enclosure—serves as a model of the world, of the cosmos, or microcosmically, of the beings of nature. Essential to such a definition of space is the ritualized means by which to fix the centers of sacredness. A ritually defined center, whether the fire at the center of the Plains tipi or the *sipapu* (Earth Navel) within the Pueblo *kiva*, expresses not just a mathematically and architecturally fixed point, but is also taken to be the actual center of the world.

In the American Southwest, where a sedentary agricultural culture fostered the evolution of an ancient architecture, we may see vividly the way in which space and history interact to produce a sacredness of place. Behind this ceremonialization of space is, as art historian Vincent Scully has observed, the demanding presence of the Pueblo Indians' antagonist, which is also their beloved mother and consort, the arid Southwestern terrain. Scully wrote:

> Long ago it began to dry up, step by step, hardly perceptibly, with many shifts and starts. The Pueblos fought that process with every resource at their command, with terracing and canals, and with magic—with everything that could be reasoned out about the forces that shape reality as it could be known. So slow was the process of desiccation that the ceremonial pattern seemed always about to catch up with it if perhaps one more factor could be involved. Hence it grew elaborate, directing the actions of every critical day, perhaps of every moment of life, and erupting always in communal ceremonies of enormous power. So strong their shapes and songs, so reasoned into strength over the centuries, that they indeed seem always to be about to accomplish what their participants desire: nothing esoteric, only more life and growth for all living things.

The Puebloan peoples of the American Southwest ritualized their relationship to the natural world around them. This symbiosis is fundamental to their architecture as well, for the environment is an implacable catalyst in the kind of shelter primal people create for themselves. The balance between the artificial and the so-called natural can be clearly seen in the architecture of the ancient Pueblo settlements, as well as those still inhabited today. Scully believes that the relationship between environment and human architectural imagination is of paramount importance in understanding a culture. "All human construction involves a relationship between the natural and the man-made. That relationship physically shapes the human cultural environment. In his-

torical terms, the character of that relationship is a major in-
dication of the character of a culture as a whole." It tells us
how the human beings who made it thought of themselves
in relation to the rest of the creation. . . . Do their buildings
contrast with the forms of the earth or do they echo them? It
tells us how they think about space.

The Greeks, offended by the natural rudeness of "primitive" ideas, revolted from the calculated symbiosis of the
non-Greeks whom they called "barbarians"—due to the fact
that their unfamiliar speech sounded like a mere *babble* to
Hellenic ears.* The Greek temple is an expression of the
man-conceived divinity—and not a response to nature's divinity. It is heroic; it confronts and balances nature's shapes
but it is not part of them. Greek architecture is a symbol of
Western man's attempt to escape from nature. All subsequent Western civilizations have lived with that dubious
and dangerous conception of freedom from nature. The architecture of the West makes an exoticism out of place just as
animals in zoos and plants in botanical gardens make an
alien curiosity of the beings of nature.

The American Indian has an entirely different view of humanity and nature from that of the Greek heritage. For primal peoples, because the landscape itself is sacred it therefore embodies a divinity that it shares with everything that
is part of nature, including human beings, animals, plants,
rocks . . . everything.

Benjamin Lee Whorf tells us, in his study of Hopi mentality, that these Indians of central Arizona have no special
names for types of buildings nor for the various rooms of a
building except the single term *yê-mòkvi*, meaning equally
"inner room" and "cavern." *Tê-wi*, meaning both "setback"
and "ledge," is derived from the so-called setback of a building and the ledge of a mountainside. Even the term *kiva* (the

---

* The Sanskrit word for stammer is *barbarah*; in Italian it is *balbettare*—the
initial *balb* being related to the *barb* of "barbarous."

ceremonial chamber of the Hopi) is not a definitive architectural term but a corruption of the Hopi word *ki-he*, which
means a building of *any* kind and doesn't specifically designate that very special, singular, and holy place where the
tribe's ceremonial life is centered. "It would seem that buildings and mountains are all one for the Hopi. Man-made
structures are works of nature, too, no different in that from
the home of the bees." (Scully) Man is part of nature and
therefore his architecture is also part of nature and reflects
the environment in which it evolves.

We should not understand by this, however, the kind of
philosophy that architects such as Frank Lloyd Wright
championed with his concept of being true to "the nature of
materials," etc. Hopi towns are not really concerned with fit-
ting in with nature, as so many Western romantic buildings
have tried to do. They *are* nature. But their resemblance to
the shapes of the earth is not coincidental. Architecture to
the Hopi is both an act of reverence and a congruence of terrain, materials, and tribal sensibility.

It is generally agreed that originally the various Southwestern villages, like Mesoamerican settlements, were ceremonial centers and not domesticities (except for a resident
priest clan). Only gradually did the huts of farmers and cus-
todians begin to form a living circle around the great religious plaza where the agriculture-oriented ceremonies were
performed. The building became an exacting framework for
rituals.

Alfonso Ortiz, the Native American anthropologist, has
indicated that the plaza of Tewa San Juan makes use of all
the major elements of the ancient "Great Kiva" found at sites
like Mesa Verde, Chetro Ketl, and Aztec. The plaza takes
cognizance of the four sacred mountains in the four sacred
directions, with four sacred hills standing before them along
the same axes. Visible from San Juan Pueblo are the horned
Truchas Peaks, which the Tewa Indians of the village call

Rock Horn Mountain, and which Ortiz identifies as San Juan's sacred mountain of the east, upon which the long axis of its largest plaza is exactly oriented. When the long files of dancers fill that sacred space, the architectural pattern is complete; the natural and the artificial together frame and encourage the human ritual act which provides sustenance and blessedness. "All is one," Scully concludes.

Humanity is harmoniously fused with the natural world through the ritualization of space.

This primal architecture is an intensification of nature and an art form that has resulted from the application of human intelligence in response to a unique environmental conception. Yet it has been largely dismissed as accidental and arbitrary until recently, when scholars like Scully and Bernard Rudofsky have come to recognize the philosophy and practical disciplines of primal builders as exceptional and untapped sources of inspiration for industrial people.

The wisdom to be derived from this primal architecture goes far beyond economic and aesthetic consideration—though these elements are very considerable in and for themselves—and touches the far tougher problem of how to live in our seemingly "unnatural" world, of how to recover our relationships to the earth both in the parochial sense and in the metaphysical scope of things.

EARTH PLANS AND ASTRAL SPACES

The architectural symbiosis of the American Southwest is perfectly reflected in the spatial schemes of most American Indian cultures. In his controversial examination of Plains mentality, Hyemeyohsts Storm has spoken about the Medicine Wheel—an architectural phenomenon that has long mystified historians and ethnologists.*

---

*For a highly critical view of Storm's book, see Rupert Costo's "Seven Arrows Desecrates Cheyenne," in Literature of the American Indians, edited by Abraham Chapman, pp. 149–51.

Among the People, a child's first Teaching is of the Four Great Powers of the Medicine Wheel. To the North on the Medicine Wheel is found Wisdom. The Color of the Wisdom of the North is White, and its Medicine Animal is the Buffalo. The South is represented by the Sign of the Mouse, and its Medicine Color is Green. The South is the place of Innocence and Trust, and for perceiving closely our nature of heart. In the West is the Sign of the Bear. The West is the Looks-Within Place, which speaks of the Introspective nature of man. The Color of this Place is Black. The East is marked by the Sign of the Eagle. It is the Place of Illumination, where we can see things clearly far and wide. Its Color is the Gold of the Morning Star.

Humanity is placed within this complex network of space, sensibility, color, and wisdom. "At birth," Storm writes, "each of us is given a particular Beginning Place within these Four Great Directions on the Medicine Wheel. This Starting Place gives us our first way of perceiving things, which will then be our easiest and most natural way throughout our lives."

Native American thought is inclined to employ spatial metaphors to describe the unity of everything in the cosmos. "Once this spiritual vision of the cosmos is recognized," historian J. Donald Hughes has commented, "the Indian attitude toward the land itself becomes understandable. The land was the gift of the domain of powerful beings. Certain locations, such as mountains and lakes, served as especially important points of contact with these spirits or forces." These places became shrines, exceptional centers of power. The Indians' relationship to the world is thus structured by *sacred* geography. Holy people tend to treat the human mind, the human body, and the whole world of nature as a single integrated organism. The Indian has a very strong and pervasive sense of place, and does not look at space as a possession. The land belongs to the past and the future, and it will be the home of the children and their children after them. Tecumseh and a few other great leaders had the vision of a whole continent given to *all* Indians, and epitomized the Indian feeling for land in the famous words, "Sell the earth? Why not sell the air, the clouds, the great sea?"

The manipulation of earthly space recapitulates the workings of cosmic space. Therefore in the great ceremonial Camp-Circle of the Sun Dance of the Plains Indians, in the architecture of the Sun Lodge itself, there is a carefully prescribed master plan that is not a matter of simply accommodating rank and bestowing places of honor, but is also a reflection of a cosmic design and rhythm that reverberates through every aspect of the American Indian relationship to the earth, to nature, and, ultimately, to the conception of place.

The conclusion of astronomer Ray Williamson and his colleagues who studied old ruins of North America was that "Native Americans wove scientific knowledge of the heavens into the fabric of their daily lives." Their spatial sensibility was not limited to geographical place but included astonishingly accurate astronomical calculations that were ritualized architecturally. Writing in *The Smithsonian*, Williamson reported that "much of the art and the architecture of American Indians of a millennium ago can be better understood in relation to celestial events." It was a field expedition's effort to determine to what extent certain Indians of the Southwest had incorporated astronomical alignments into their architecture. Twelve months of research provided some startling answers to that question.

> It was the time of the summer solstice—an event which we believed the builders of Hovenweep Castle [New Mexico] had understood. Our measurements and computer analysis had suggested that the narrow port in the sandstone-block wall was so placed that at sunset the last rays of the sun would pierce it, announcing the turning of the year in a way that all could see . . . sooner than we expected, a shaft of sun-

light penetrated the aperture. At sunset it fell precisely on
the corner where the northern and eastern walls joined. . . .
Hundreds of years before, the inhabitants of the castle had
observed the event we had just watched, and had known
that the sun's daily path across the sky would now shift
slowly toward the south and the seasons would continue in
their endless rotation.

Thus the sacredness of space is not limited in the primal
mentality to the relation of place to earthly directions and
mythic history and characters, but is also closely and accu-
rately related to heavenly movement. "The original 'D'
tower of Hovenweep Castle," wrote Williamson, "was constructed in about A.D. 1200. Several generations later more
rooms were added, including the chamber where we observed the solstice sunset." During the construction process,
the Anasazi (a Navajo term meaning "the ancient ones"—
the ancestors of the Pueblo people of today) incorporated
two special ports, or sighting holes, into the walls, one
aligned to the summer solstice sunset on June 21, the other
to the winter solstice sunset on December 21. In addition,
they designed the outside doorway of the castle so that its
jambs align to sunset on the two equinoxes (roughly March
21 and September 21), when day equals night in length.
These facts led Williamson and his colleagues to believe that
the ancestors of the Pueblo people seven hundred years ago
may have employed a precise spatially oriented calendar for
planting, harvesting, and ritual observances.

The primal conception of astronomical motion is essentially spatial—and not mathematical and abstract. Therefore, for
instance, at the Hopi pueblos, the times for ceremonies and
for agricultural activities are determined by watching the
sun rise and set in precise relation to the mountainous skyline. Each important day has a peak or notch in the skyline
named for it. When the rising or setting sun appears or disappears at the precise and appointed landmark, it is time to

perform the ceremony or to begin planting. This interrelationship of events, astronomical motion, and geographical space integrates the Native American conception of humanity's place in nature to such an extent that it is impossible to speak of space or place without bringing to bear numerous sacred and metaphoric ideals. And this sacredness of places ranges the entire Western Hemisphere.

Among the thousands of stone rings situated on the eastern slopes of the Rocky Mountains are a few large, complex structures known as Medicine Wheels, already described by Hyemeyohsts Storm. "Laid out by the early tribes before the white man appeared in the West," Ray Williamson stated, "the function of the wheels has long been a mystery and local Indians used to disclaim any knowledge of who built them or what their purpose might be" insofar as such Medicine Wheels are a central aspect of Plains' secret rituals. From observations made in 1972 and 1973, astronomer John Eddy of the High Altitude Observatory in Boulder, Colorado, discovered that the Bighorn Medicine Wheel (in Bighorn National Forest of northern Wyoming, where the observer has an unobstructed view of the eastern and western horizons) is aligned to the sunrise and sunset positions of the summer solstice sun. Thus, Williamson concludes, "certainly a 'cosmic' point of view permeated the thinking of Native Americans in historic times. The Medicine Wheel, the kiva, and the observatory are merely artifacts of their struggle to understand the world they inhabited." That understanding, however, does not indicate that these first Americans were distinctly like Western thinkers, but contrarily, it suggests that they possessed an accurate but quite different and alternative way of seeing the cosmos and their relationship to it.

"So far as the [primal] man carries out technical activities in space," writes Heinz Werner, "so far as he measures distances, steers his canoe, hurls his spear at a certain target, and so on, his space as a field of action, as a pragmatic space, does not differ in its structure from our own. But when [primal] man makes this space a subject of representation and of reflective thought, there arises a specifically primordial idea differing radically from any [Western] intellectualized version. The idea of space, for [primal] man, even when systematized, is syncretically bound up with the subject. It is a notion much more affective and concrete than the abstract space of the man of [Western] culture. . . . It is not so much objective, measurable, and abstract in character."

Primal mentality does not formulate a *system* of space: an abstract postulation of linear laws that govern the cosmos. Ernst Cassirer (1946) has noted:

> Ethnologists show us that [primal] tribes usually are gifted with an extraordinarily sharp perception of space. A native of these tribes has an eye for all the nicest details of his environment. He is extremely sensitive to every change in the position of the common objects of his surroundings. Even under very difficult circumstances he will be able to find his way. When rowing or sailing he follows with the greatest accuracy all the turns of the river that he goes up and down. But upon closer examination we discover to our surprise that in spite of this facility there seems to be a strange lack in his apprehension of space. If you ask him to give you a general description, a delineation of the course of the river he is not able to do so. If you wish him to draw a map of the river and its various turns he seems not even to understand your question.

The primal experience of space is not linear; it does not fit into the grid patterns so common in Western spatial orientation. The abstraction of space in the West—like the forms of perspective described earlier—is an atomization of space that provides us with loci—with points in a determined space—but not with the actual *experience* of space as natural and sensual phenomena. The primal mind knows space experientially. This affective relationship with space of the primal person, however, does not limit his experience to pragmatic spatial actions, for he sees space as *the sacred theatre of his life* and the ritual umbilical cord that forever connects him to his divine parent, the Earth.

6

MOTION

> All living creatures are constantly consummating their own
> internal rhythm.
>
> —JEAN D'UDINE

The body is an organ of expression. It is not simply a utilitarian organization of limbs, nor is it the millstone of the disembodied Christian soul. It is not only the machinery of procreation, digestion, and other functional activities; it is also an organ of expression—perhaps the most vivid facility for the expression of immediately experienced ideas and feelings. It is the place where humanity achieves the ritualization of motion in an art form called "dance." The body is the organism in which motion makes visible the sacred forms of life itself. Our bodies live through motion. And thus motion is the most important and pervasive means by which primal peoples celebrate living.

As Susanne K. Langer (1957) observed, "Strange as it may seem, the evolution of the dance as a high art belongs to prehistory. At the dawn of civilization, dance had already reached a degree of perfection that no other art or science could then match." But the choreographic achievement of primal peoples was largely dismissed by post-Aristotelian societies, for whom dance was a savage expression lacking discipline and intelligence. Until the founding of a highly mechanized European form of dancing, called ballet, dance was rarely given serious attention as an art in the West, and was, as an activity of the mortified flesh, rejected by Chris-

133

tianity and given no subsidy. Christianity was thus the only world church that actively abhorred dancing and refused to include it in its orthodox services after a brief period during which it was unofficially used in miracle plays and other religious theatrics.

For primal peoples, however, "worship is dance," Langer concludes; "they are tribes of dancers."

The Indian song-dance for rain is the prayer of a whole people for the regeneration of their *spiritual bodies*. Wind is the precursor of the rain, but before the ceremonial performers can become the rain they must first become the wind. The great prayer that follows is the dramatic climax of the Navajo "Night Chant," and it represents for the Navajo people a source of power and meaning far greater than anything yet offered to the Indian by Western civilization.

The prayer is addressed to the thunderbird of pollen and is carried into the wind-swollen sky that is called *the house of storms*:

> Tsegihi!
> House made of the dawn,
> House made of evening light . . .
> Dark cloud is at the door . . .
> The zigzag lightning stands high up on it.
> Male divinity!
> Your offering I make.

In this fusion of dance, song, and music is "art" before art exists. Nothing in this richly metaphoric ritual of the Navajos is the equivalent of the West's self-conscious idealizations of art and beauty. The purpose of the "Night Chant" is curiously practical from the Western standpoint, despite the fact that it abounds in subtle expressiveness and visual eloquence. Though it possesses an important relevance to the whole lifestyle and matrix of the Navajo world, the "Night Chant" is not the utterance of a disembodied, lost soul suffering the torments of original sin and damnation. It is, instead, a highly physical event concerned with a practical reality, specifically a curative ceremony enacted by a holy person ("singer") to remedy the ills of a tribesperson ("patient"). But in the use of the word "patient" (which is generally applied to the person who sponsors the ceremony and pays a commission to the holy people), the significance of the illness from the Indian viewpoint is entirely lost. For the "disease" to be cured is an ailment of the "spiritual body" that has mysteriously lost touch with the cosmos—has faltered in its perceptual kinship with nature.

The idea that spirituality can be associated with the body is extremely remote from the white man's belief in the dichotomy of mind and body, spirit and flesh. It was until very recently inconceivable in the world of Christianity and Judaism that there could be any relationship between spiritual and physical reality. To most non-Indians dancing is a form of mindless amusement. It was not until the turn of the century that dance was evolved into an art form by people like Isadora Duncan, Martha Graham, Erick Hawkins, Lester Horton, José Limon, and Merce Cunningham. Until then body movement possessed a very humble and static existence in Western civilizations. It was so detested by both church and synagogue that it was officially prohibited after a brief but important expressive use in early religious ceremonies, like the Christian "Circle of the Angels" and David's dance before the altar of the synagogue.

It is difficult after centuries of belief in the mortification of the flesh (and the celebration of the "eternal soul") for most Western people to grasp the possibility of a spiritual body in which spirit and flesh are unified. The Indian concept of harmony among all things is so alien to the West that Westerners cannot conceive of a spiritual conviction that is communicated through dance—a unique expressive act in which, more than any other, there is immediacy and a perfect unity of thought and feeling. As Indians have often stated to the bewilderment of whites, dancing is the "breath-of-life" made visible. This concept of the breath-of-life is discovered everywhere in the unique spiritual world of Indians; in the ceremonial stem of the sacred pipe, in the heart line of animals imprinted on pottery, in the rites of inhaling the first light of day and the conferring of blessing by exhaling into the hands of a devotee. All these symbolic images and gestures are associated with the wind and with the breathing of the living cosmos—the visible motion of the power that invests everything in existence.

When ethnologist Washington Matthews was collecting histories and legends among the Navajos in the 1890s, he was told something by a holy man that made a deep impression. "It is the wind that gave them life," the old man whispered, the "them" referring to First Man and First Woman, the Navajo Adam and Eve, to whom the wind imparted the breath-of-life. "It is the wind that comes out of our mouths now that gives us life," the holy man continued as he gestured to his chest and throat. "When this ceases to blow—we die." Then he held his wrinkled hand to the light of the oil lamp and gazed at his fingertips. "In the skin of our fingers we see the trail of the wind . . ." and he then made a circular motion to indicate the whirlwind that left its imprint in the whorls at the tips of the human finger. "It shows us where the wind blew when our ancestors were created."

The breath-of-life and its associations with song, rhythm, dance, and motion are central to Indian culture. It is a theme that runs elaborately through every Indian tradition, illuminated by the ceremonies, the music, and the dances of American Indian tribes. It is also a conceptual metaphor that is the background of the religious viewpoint of Native Americans despite the fact that there has been great diversity among the tribes and abundant influence from European religious forms after the invasion of 1492.

If you agree with those who believe that action came before conjecture in human societies, then you will recognize in bodily movement humanity's most fundamental and expressive act—evolved to a sublime achievement long before the emergence of the first civilizations of the West. Dance is the inclination of primal peoples to idealize action as a magical force. There is substantial physiological basis behind this viewpoint. We are born with organs of perception that provide us with our only means of experiencing the world. These organs include not only the senses of smell, sight, hearing, taste, and touch, but also a sense of balance and of rotation, which the semicircular canals in the inner ear reveal to us through successive impulses sent to the brain. In addition we possess a kinesthetic sense, which operates through little understood receptors in our muscle tissues and through our tactile sensitivity to pressure and texture, and which helps us realize when we are moving and on what kind of surface we are moving. From birth we are taught to recognize the ways in which the movements of our bodies work for us practically: swimming, driving, writing, eating. But bodily movement has other functions—and primal people are as aware of them as they are of the purely practical ways in which motion serves us. Every sentient state expresses itself in movements that are not necessarily utilitarian or representational, but that nevertheless reflect the specific quality of the ideas and feelings that cause them. The relationship between sentience and movement affects everything from the expression in our eyes to the flow of adrenaline in our bloodstream. In its most fundamental form this spontaneous link between sentience and movement is called dance—a direct, nonverbal, unreasoned assertion of ideas and sentience expressed in forms of motion. From this fact it becomes clear that dance is an extremely powerful force in human experience, especially if we live in a society in which less importance is given to words than to actions.

Martha Graham has made no secret of her debt to the Indians of the Southwest. Photographer Barbara Morgan made the following remarks: "I had just seen one of Martha's concerts. I can't exactly remember whether it was *Primitive Mysteries* or *Frontier*, but I was very excited and it aroused memories of my experiences in the Southwest. So I asked Martha very directly, 'By any chance have you been influenced by the Indian and Spanish dance ceremonies in the American Southwest?' She said to me: 'Absolutely, that's one of the greatest inspirations in my entire life.' "

Graham was not the only choreographer to be influenced by the Kachina dances of the American Southwest. Erick Hawkins who grew up in Colorado, Lester Horton who knew the Indian rituals and performed adaptations of them during his early solo career, Ted Shawn and his famous men's group, and the Mexican Indian choreographer José Limon also saw and admired Indian ceremonies that had an essential impact on their work and that of their students. It is reasonable, as a matter of fact, to attribute much of the thrust of the rebellion against Western ballet and the evolution of so-called modern dance to the influence of American Indian rites on the American choreographers of the early part of the twentieth century.

THE KACHINA DANCES

These Kachina dances, which Graham and several other major choreographers saw in America's Southwestern region, are the public part of an elaborate religious lifestyle. The Kachinas of the Southwest exist in over 250 iconographic forms best known by whites in the form of painted wooden dolls. These dolls are given to Pueblo children so they can be displayed in homes to help them learn to identify the various Kachinas. The dolls are learning tools, not sacred objects. But once the members of the tribal societies who "impersonate" the Kachinas in ceremonial events don their costumes and masks and take up their paraphernalia, they become sacred reflections of the powers of Kachinas and may not be touched or involved in human conversation or any other form of exchange. The fact that Kachinas are sacred doesn't obstruct their potential for actions that are grotesque, outrageous, and highly humorous—all such qualities exist in the great sacred rites of American Indians.

The rites of the Pueblo tribes arose anonymously from the spiritual life of an entire people, and are so complexly interwoven with that people's iconographic values that they have a pervasive depth of meaning to every member of the tribe. In the West dance, like all the arts, has become elitist insofar as its impact is understood fully only by a rather small group of initiated spectators. This process of secularization is particularly visible in the history of dance in the West. We can clearly see the shift from the mystic acts of tribes to the organized ceremonies of churches, and then the self-serving spectacles commissioned by the princes of the Middle Ages. We are able to see how the ritual forms of primal people often outlive the spiritual viewpoint they originally contained, and how the motivating forces of dance change from tribal expressiveness to the eccentric creation of an individual choreographer.

In Europe, and especially in Italy, until the middle of the fifteenth century, the Church was virtually the only patron of art, and this largely anonymous art was required to make statements about Catholic beliefs—morality, cosmology, and absolute truths. The Renaissance grandees who later dominated the art market had very little interest in philosophies, but were inclined to use art to promote their own reputations and to heighten their prestige. Each patron endeavored to commission works that would outshine those sponsored by rivals. It is clear in the relationship between the art of the Church and that of the grandees that the nature and purpose of expression changed drastically. That change is even greater when we consider the transformation of tribal rites into ecclesiastical art. And the most drastic change of all was the transformation of the art created for Renaissance patrons into art produced almost entirely with the motive of self-expression.

The rituals created by Western individuals have often described a personal vision, but they have also served nationalistic causes. There have been numerous efforts among black choreographers to reconstruct the African experience: notably in the works of Pearl Primus, but also in the dances of Katherine Dunham, Jean-Leon Destiné, and the choreographers of the Alvin Ailey Company. In the years following the Great Depression, choreographers like Anna Sokolow and the New Dance Trio attempted to ritualize their radical political viewpoints. But whether the intention of a choreographer is tribal, social, political, or highly personal, the process of ritualizing experience is essentially the same. With a Western historical perspective it is possible, for instance, to grasp how and why the competitive flamboyance of the era of Charles XIII of France was central to the formative character of court dancing and ballet. And in more recent times it is equally clear that the Freudian emphasis upon the interior world influenced the emergence of modern dance and the cult of personality that Isadora Duncan came to symbolize. This relationship between the driving forces of culture and the forms of dance demonstrates the crucial way in which human experience is ritualized.

THE POWER OF MOTION

Dance is clearly an extremely important and powerful force in human experience. Beyond its purely expressive powers there is also the highly contagious nature of bodily movement. Yawning is the most obvious example of this; so is the desire to stretch when we see someone else stretching.

Because of the inherent contagion of motion, which makes onlookers feel in their own bodies the exertion they see in others, the dancer is able to convey nonverbally, even non-symbolically, the most intangible and metaphysical experiences, ideas, and sentience.

The body is capable of communicating in its own bodily manner. It is only since the beginning of the twentieth century that the power of dance as a communicative medium has been fully appreciated, but primal peoples have understood and focused on this affectiveness of dance since long before the rise of the earliest civilizations. When we consider how powerfully movement influences all of us, it isn't difficult to understand why primal people regard an action as the embodiment of a mysterious force. They believe that dance can shape the circumstances of nature if it can focus its contagious powers on animals and supernaturals. This premise of sympathetic magic is at the root of most ceremonial use of dance. The imitation of an animal (essentially in movements, but also in costume) has an influence upon the animal itself. This practice, called homeopathic ritual, is the basis of most hunting and fertility rites. It probably resulted from a long history of less complex usages of bodily motion until it was determined that actions of a certain kind were highly effective: depicting the pursuit and slaying of an animal might influence the animal powers to sacrifice one of their kind so human beings might eat and survive, etc. At such a point, thought and action are fused in a form unknown in the West except, perhaps, in the specialized process that is separated from the practical activities of life and called "art."

In this effort to move closer to the centers of power in nature, primal people often imitate and transform themselves into things of the natural world that invest them with vision and strength. Tribal people receive power through songs. Through their dances they touch unknown and unseen elements which they sense in the world around them, but over which they have no control. It is perhaps an error to speak of the imitation of animals, because the dancer's actions are designed not for emulation but for transformation. Modern dancers have consciously rediscovered this same process: they do not simply *perform* the movements of a choreographer—they *become* the movements, through intense kinesthetic projection of ideas and sentience as pure bodily expression. It is a process difficult to describe as it takes place in tribal rites, but it is essentially the nature of dance as an expressive, nondecorative form. When we see this process in a work by Erick Hawkins we are at a loss to describe how it happens. For primal peoples, this process of being transformed into movement is easy.

Ideas and feelings are merged in the spiritual body. Words—chanted, sung, or spoken—are valued in rituals primarily for the reaction they produce within the singer rather than for any effect they might have on others. The first stage of ritual is almost always the rise of the singer on his or her own song to a plane of power—a place of contact with the forces that move the cosmos. The words and sounds of a song are only the small, visible aspect of a far greater mystery that lies beneath and beyond syntactical speech. For this reason, the nature of ritual songs requires the comprehension of a larger idea, a sound or a word or two that convey something far wider and truer than what is actually spoken or sounded.

No one knows for certain just how song and dance originated, but there is in all animals, including of course humans, a relationship between intense feeling and involuntary bodily movement and utterance. Due to the stresses of movement upon the belly and upon the diaphragm, there is a tendency for vocalization. It is the kind of noise people make when they sit down or get up, or when they are surprised or dismayed. The contractive movement of many ritual dances also results in the forced exhalation of breath, causing vocal sounds. The variety of movement, accent, and intensity produces many different kinds of sounds. It is possible that some of the songs which accompany dances are the result of such vocal utterances that involuntarily occur during dancing. Whatever the origins of song and its physical relationships to dance, we know from ethnologists that song and dance are intrinsic in most primal cultures—the dancers accompany themselves with sounds of rhythmic accents produced by clapping and stomping. It is often conjectured that once the energies of the dance accelerated, making self-accompaniment difficult, the beat and vocal sounds were picked up by a less active dancer or bystanders who eventually became the "orchestra." In this way, dance emerged as a form distinct from music in the ritual arts.

The outward rusticity of primal behavior makes Western people devise a self-serving ideal of themselves as civilized, which sets them widely apart from other peoples. They are inclined to forget that the same impulses which give form to primal people are active in all cultures despite diversities. The twentieth-century Western mind is a product of its gradual withdrawal from an awareness of nature and its place in it. Westerners believe that nature serves them and that divine intention makes them the dominant beings of the world. It was with this "manifest destiny" in mind that Europeans assumed their right to possess the ancient lands of other peoples. Such primal peoples live among animals and vegetation constantly in close contact with the sources of nourishment and death, understanding their environment and expressing their ideas and feelings in terms of the natural world, rather than some curiously unnatural idealization they have constructed about themselves in relation to the world.

The response of primal people to their environment is largely ritualistic. Such ritualization of experience is itself a type of idealization of the relationship of humanity and its surroundings, but in a form that modern Westerners find less effective than their hope to neutralize (rather than to ritualize) nature. Rituals tend to deal with ambiguity on the level of ambiguity—in the way that art deals with reality. On the other hand, the "civilized" viewpoint is inclined to turn ambiguity into certitude and orthodoxy. The central method for this transposition from a world of essences to a world of objects and appearances, as philosophers Ernst Cassirer and Susanne K. Langer have indicated, is through the use of words as the definitive framework of realism. Langer (1942) informs us:

> Words are certainly our most important instruments of expression, our most characteristic, universal and enviable tools in the conduct of life. Speech is the mark of humanity. It is the normal terminus of thought. We are apt to be so impressed with its symbolistic mission that we regard it as the only important expressive act, and assume that all other activity must be practical in an animalian way, or else irrational—playful, or atavistic (residual) past recognition. But in fact, speech is the natural outcome of only one kind of symbolic process. These are transformations of experience in the human mind that have quite different overt endings. They end in acts that are neither practical nor communicative, though they may be both effective and communal; I mean the actions we call *ritual*.

Ritual is a motional, symbolic transformation of experiences that no other medium of expression can adequately contain. Because it springs from a primary human need, it is a spontaneous activity that arises without self-consciousness, without adaptation to either a pragmatic or a conscious purpose. Its growth is undesigned in the sense that primal architecture is "undesigned." Its patterns, for all their intricacy, merely express the social process of a unique people who are largely unconscious of the social structure in which they live. Ritual is never successfully imposed upon a people. When such missionary efforts are made (like the introduction of Catholicism to the Yaqui Indians of the Southwest), the imposed ideology is thoroughly assimilated into preexisting ritual forms and thus neutralized.

The province of ritual, like motion and dance, has been continually assaulted as mindless and compulsive because it does not sustain the certitude and orthodoxy of the language-bound mentality of civilized peoples. Freud saw rites as acts that must be performed out of sheer inward compulsion. It is now apparent that ritual acts are often the spontaneous transformation of external as well as internal experiences. A good example of ritual as a form of social accommodation is visible in the *Booger Dance* of the Big Cove band of the Eastern Cherokees. In this ritual, which is not quite the same as any other Cherokee ceremony, we discover a dramatic record of the anxiety of the tribe, a strong reaction against the symbol of the white invaders, and an expression of fear in dealing with the Western world that surrounds the Big Cove settlement. The *Booger Dance* fuses the invasion of the whites to the spiritual forces of nature with which the Cherokee people had learned to cope successfully, therefore making the existence of white men somehow less alien and threatening. The Cherokee believe that they cannot politically deal with the white invaders, but feel completely competent to cope with the same whites when transformed by ritual into mythical animals and grotesquely obscene creatures that invade the Indian settlement in a ritual performance. In other words, the Indians do not feel sufficiently powerful politically and pragmatically to deal with white people. They do, however, feel competent to do so through ritual—the means by which, at a much earlier time, they successfully transmuted their very harsh geographical environment into a familiar ritual context through which they could assert influence and with which they could ultimately achieve harmony.

The *Booger Dance* perfectly ritualizes an ugly and difficult experience for the Cherokee Indians. It describes the coming of outsiders, who are changed into Boogers, who intrude in the midst of tribal life uninvited, seeking something to exploit. In the dance, the Indians tolerate the invaders until, their desires gratified, the whites leave. Thus the white man's existence, his unmannerly insistences, and his intrusion into the Cherokee home circle at the height of social festivities become grotesque and comic aspects of a ritual experience. But the ritual does not indulge in wishful thinking—or it would not be successful. The whites are realistically depicted as aggressive and dominant intruders, but these characteristics are transformed into grotesque parody. The Boogers have obscene names and wear imitation sex organs made of gourds, which are filled with water that sprays in every direction as they chase Indian women. When the Boogers are asked what they want, they first say "GIRLS!" Told politely that Indian women do not like Boogers, they then say they want "TO FIGHT!" The Cherokee leader explains that Indians are peaceful and do not want to fight, but that they are willing to dance with the Boogers. The invaders accept the invitation to dance and use the opportunity to abuse the native women who join them in the dance but who remain aloof from the Boogers' simulation of sexual aggression. Then the Boogers finally depart, having been successfully neutralized by this complex ritual action. The Cherokees, now jubilant, celebrate their cultural victory over the race that has militaristically defeated them.

The *Booger Dance* contradicts much of what Freud and his followers have assumed about ritual acts. These ceremonies are not necessarily unconscious outpourings of feelings into shouting, prancing, and rolling on the ground, like a baby's tantrum. For as soon as an expressive act is intentionally performed without compulsion, it is no longer simply "self-expressive," in the narrow, psychopathic sense. Instead, it becomes logically expressive, but not necessarily in the kind of logic conveyed by words. Neither is the *Booger Dance* simply a set of emotional signs; rather it is a metaphor for an *entire experience*. Instead of completing the natural history of emotions, the dance denotes feelings and ambiguously summons these feelings to mind without actuating them.*

If the *Booger Dance* of the Cherokee Indians—which was at first automatic—is repeatedly performed for the sheer joy of expression, it becomes aesthetic at that point. Anger enjoyed in being acted out consciously is not mere compulsive anger. The ultimate product of such articulation of tensions is not a simple emotion, but a complex and relatively permanent attitude that expresses itself through a variety of forms typical of the culture which produces it. As it develops toward an aesthetic character, ritual expresses feelings and ideas in the formal rather than the purely physiological sense. The word *expression*, as I use it here in relation to ritual, dance, and motion, is a deliberate conveyance of values—and not simply an emotional outburst or a public tantrum.

The process of civilization may be contradictory to the process of art and ritual. In civilization, the power of these activities is gradually displaced and abandoned as people discover a Western conviction of cause and effect, and pursue the control of nature by methods which alter the causal circumstances of their essential existence as a people. At such a time, the power of actions and images ceases to be a prime object of the community. Dance—and motion generally—persists but it expresses itself on the basis of other aims

---

* A comprehensive study of the process of ritualization and dancing may be found in Jamake Highwater's *Dance: Rituals of Experience*, 1978, and *Ritual of the Wind: North American Indian Ceremonies, Music, and Dances*, 1977.

and principles. In southern France, for instance, a folk dance called the *farandole* is still performed. It is a labyrinth-patterned dance common in much European folk choreography. Its patterns derive from an ancient symbol found on Greek coins.

The snakelike winding of the *farandole* of Provence, an ancient French colony of Greece, closely resembles a journey to the middle of the labyrinth. This Greek labyrinth pattern was a vision of the passage of a dead person to the land of the afterlife, a passage fraught with danger from evil powers. In performing a funeral dance toward the middle of a manmade labyrinth, the ancients were demonstrating that people possess the force to direct certain events of nature through sympathetic rites. This winding *farandole* was a means of mimicking the spirit of the dead person and helping it on its way. Today, the farmers of Provence still perform the *farandole* but without any conscious purpose other than the enjoyment of music and movement. In this case, the expressive form of the ritual has been abandoned. What remains is neither art nor ritual but something else: an entertainment, a game.

The rituals of primal peoples are products of hundreds of generations, a slow selective process by which certain actions are retained through repetition. These rites possess strong magic. They do not easily vanish and leave only a game (a seemingly purposeless pattern of exuberant physical movements) except under specific duress and over a great period of time. Sooner or later in the forward push of Western civilizations toward a totally controlled and verbalized construct of nature, a mimetic dance form makes its appearance—a dumb show, a substitution for words. Out of this pragmatic dance mime comes the separation of drama, dance, and music. Ultimately, not only power and expressivity, but also dance motion itself pass from the rituals of civilization, and a purely literary drama of ideas comes into existence. This is the basis of much Western naive realism.

The forward plunge of Western civilization, which some still look upon as progress, has brought the impulse to express feelings too rigidly under the domination of reason, and this, in turn, has caused the Western mind to think of itself predominantly as a perpetual spectator of the world, afraid to create its own artistic forms because they might fall outside the conventional preconception of reality. Until very recently, Western people were very much cut off from their own bodies and from expressive activities by their own constraint and embarrassment. They lacked a body that could function in harmony with their ideas and feelings. Consequently they tended to "leave the dancing to the primitives"—thus reassuring themselves of the old Christian assessment of the body and its motion as liabilities and as a humble organism over which they possessed little if any control. Without an articulate body, without facial movement that genuinely reflects states of mind, without a torso that responds to the self and relates to external events, people cannot participate in their world or, for that matter, in their own emotional lives.

The perfectly coordinated, lavishly expressive body of the ritual dancer is unmistakably different from the prim, rather stiff, and fashionably stylized body of the ballet dancer. In the ceremonial performer, there is an idealized transparency—a configuration in which the totality of human experience is visible. The feelings intrinsic to ritual are probably no more fundamental or primitive than the loftiest sentience of any of the Western arts. The ideas inherent in ritual motion may appear at first simplistic because Western people, at least until Isadora Duncan, did not believe that something as inarticulate and fanciful as dancing could possibly convey anything profound or significant. That is perhaps true of much of the white man's dancing, which had greatly declined from its ritual purposes when contemporary dancers at the turn of the twentieth century began the arduous effort of rediscovering the potential of relating dancing to the most serious rather than the most superficial aspects of the human condition. But for primal peoples, dance perfectly and simultaneously embodies the most commonplace and the most exceptional ideals. If dance relates imperfectly to the contemporary world, and if choreographers have found it difficult to invest movement with an awareness of feelings and ideas that have evolved in the West for centuries, it is perhaps because dance was so neglected during that long evolution and did not develop that kind of relationship to the white audience which it has always had in relation to primal cultures.

As Martha Graham once noted, dance is stupendously simple, and that is what makes it so difficult for modern Western people to comprehend. The idea of the spiritual body is equally simple. If there were better words to describe such a phenomenon, perhaps it would be easier to articulate this idea, but in that case it would be doubtful that there would be any reason to talk about ritual, ceremony, dance, and motion in the first place. There is nothing really "spiritual" in the concept of the spiritual body, but there isn't another word that suggests all the qualities of nobility, loftiness of thought, intensity of ideals and feelings which we normally exclude from our connotation of *body*. The concept behind the term "spiritual body" does not envision just the anatomical body but all the still-mysterious physiology by which the body experiences itself and the world, the amplification of the senses and the puzzling process of perception and thought by which "brain" re-creates itself as "mind."

Primal people have little concern or faith in the materialism that imposes mind/brain and soul/body dichotomies. A body is all there is of us. The primal process of life is holistic and formative. It is not imprisoned in a linear *uni-verse* with

its unthinkable Copernican gears moving some pathetic, calculated clock by which only civilized Westerners are supposed to be able to tell the correct time.

The story of motion and dancing in the West is as much
an alternative vision of the events of history as is the folk
history told for generations by primal chroniclers of oral literature and national epics. Both Western and primal dancers,
however, seem to have something in common: they are both
aliens standing outside the value systems of the now dominant culture. The changes in viewpoint since the turn of the
century are connected with the current enthusiasm for dancing in the West—an unprecedented boom in the dance
world. A reappraisal of Western sex roles, of ethnocentricity,
of civilization, and of the human community have vitally altered the white man's attitude toward himself and his body.

"No form of dance is permanent," critic John Martin observed, ". . . no form of dance is definitive, ultimate . . . only
the basic principle of dance is enduring, and out of it, like
the cycle of nature itself, rises an endless succession of new
springs out of old winters."

7

SOUND

> Music is a ritual whose function is to help imperfect man be-
> come identical with "perfect nature." Such music is neither
> egocentric Romantic self-expression, nor artificial common
> sense, nor selfish pleasure, nor artificial Classical order. . . .
> Such music is not expressing man instead of nature, nor na-
> ture instead of man—but man identical with perfect nature,
> bringing us to our very best . . . real, alive, free.
> —LUCIA DLUGOSZEWSKI

Several elements used to distinguish between discursive, Logos-bound Western music and the ritualistic and Eros-oriented music of primal peoples. Then, at the beginning of the
twentieth century, the unique values of tribal music began
to overflow into compositions which the avant-garde of the
1920s called Neo-Primitive, like Igor Stravinsky's *Rite of
Spring* (1913). It is because of this contemporary revaluation
of the neglected music of nonindustrial peoples that we can
discover in today's Western music many characteristics that
previously existed only in the music of primal cultures. For
these reasons there now exist two forms of "primal" music—
the ethnological type, which is considered to be among the
earliest forms of tribal expression, and the type of individualized contemporary music of the West that attempts to reiterate aspects of ritualism at the same time that it espouses a
radical harmonic modernism.

Regardless of the influence from tribal cultures upon the
music of the dominant society, Western music remains outside the oral tradition that universally links non-Western,

tribal musical expression. This oral tradition is the most important single feature that all tribal musics have in common. The existence of this unwritten form of music makes *immediacy* its central impetus and assures a grasp of the *instance* as an intrinsic part of tribal musical mentality. Such an oral tradition in music also depends upon unwritten forms of education and cultural acquisitions and preservations. By contrast, the music of the West is perpetuated not orally but by means of a schematic musical notation. Even when composers have sought to revive ritualism in their compositions and have discarded traditional Western notation in favor of aleatory (chance) schematics which provide performers with a wide freedom in the performance of "written" music, still the conceptual tradition of Western notation dominates musical imagination. Composers still think and create in terms of that musical world accessible to them through notation. What cannot be written does not exist for them.

Another characteristic shared by the music of an oral tradition is that it is experiential rather than formal, emotional, or decorative. In this primal experientiality people of the West are likely to see utilitarianism, insofar as tribal music is filled with magical, symbolic, metaphoric, and social significance and is performed as part of a larger cultural activity. But ultimately there is no more utility in primal music than there is in the so-called abstract music of the West, which until about the eighteenth century was largely composed to celebrate Christian doctrine or to accompany the banquets of grandees, or their fireworks displays and cruises down the Thames. Nonetheless, in both the Western world and among primal peoples music holds a revered place.

Music has occupied a central position in the folk history of all nations; in the religious organizations of ancient China; in the mystical philosophy of the Pythagorean philosophers of ancient Greece; in the Vedic rites of India; and in the mythos of contemporary tribal peoples such as American Indians, Australian Aborigines, and the many African and Oceanic tribes. In the power and empirical immediacy of music, primal cultures envision not simply the immense performing magic of skilled musicians but also the conception of *sound itself* as one of the primeval forces of creation. This viewpoint is often ambiguous and metaphoric, but it can also be quite literal, as in the folk history of the Tamil peoples, which relates that the world itself was derived from the tambourine of the god.

By no means is this power and immediacy of music absent in the contemporary West, where at least one example of this kind of folk music-making is still to be found in the European music called "Noise of Darkness" performed during the Holy Week rituals of the Catholic Church. The conception of music as natural sound and as an intrinsic rather than extraneous part of nature is an abiding theme of some of our most interesting twentieth-century composers and writers— such as Richard Wagner, John Cage, Wilfred Mellers, Edgard Varèse, Béla Bartók, Olivier Messiaen, Pierre Boulez, Karlheinz Stockhausen, and Lucia Dlugoszewski. It is largely from their elaborations of primal concepts that we may grasp in Western terms the most fundamental aspects of non-Western sensibilities, for modern European and American composers (even more than painters) have vivified primal mentality and transformed the whole focus and rationale of contemporary music by their use of ritualism as an original, experimental, and highly individualized expressive idiom. Such activity among Western musicians is often a conscious reaction against the Logos-bound mentality of their own culture. Dlugoszewski has written:

Logos has dominated Western music. Yet it can never grasp all of reality, no matter how comprehensive it becomes. Still Logos is already intrinsic to all of our music: 256 cycles per second designates middle C, and an elegant 512 cycles per second designates a C an octave higher. This is the relational analytical ratio of the octave—displaying its symmetry, its transparency, its emotional purity. The grand design of Logos in Western music would be a ritual of infinite harmonious relations, correlated to a harmonically understood cosmos. But the problem of Logos lies in the fact that (at least so far) deliberate application of the purely theoretic component renders a music that is unliving and artificial.

What composers like Dlugoszewski and John Cage search for in music is what Herbert Marcuse has championed as "the aesthetic dimension" which brings about the "liberation of sensuousness from the repressive domination of reason." Make no error, however, for this is not merely a Neo-Romantic or Neo-Primitive resonance in the world of contemporary Western music, but to the contrary it is, at best, a far more fundamental issue and a far more important aspect of contemporary music-making.

Philosopher F.S.C. Northrop (1966) clarifies Marcuse's statement in terms of the modern artist's dilemma: "Unless we are protected by poetry, reality in its purely theoretical aspect is sought at the cost of losing its equally real aesthetic [primal] component, and the mind of man becomes over-stimulated while his spirit dies."

It is clear that the ancient and embattled history of Logos in its contest with Eros continues as the dominant metaphor of the distinctions between primal thinking (among artists, philosophers, and tribal peoples) and Western mentality.* Because of the repressive dominion of reason from the time of Plato onward, music has tended to be assigned pseudo-

---

* Zukav discusses a tangential elaboration of this Logos-Eros dichotomy which, though fundamentally different from the Northrop premise, complements and extends this discussion. "The difference between experience and symbol is the difference between mythos and logos. Logos imitates, but can never replace, experience . . . mythos points toward experience, but it does not replace experience. According to [David] Finkelstein, a language of mythos, a language which alludes to experience but does not attempt to replace it or to mold our perception of it is the true language of physics."

functions in Western society—becoming a kind of mathematics, a kind of engineering, a form of self-expressive psychology, a substitute for purely linguistic projections which have nothing fundamentally to do with music as sound or as part of nature but attempt, instead, to turn music into some kind of discursive and syntactical "language of tonalities."

"What was evident in all the arts," Dlugoszewski writes, "has also been true of the last three decades of musical history: ever more ruthless upheavals and ferocious contradictions—what someone wittily described as composers 'calling each others liars.' " The upheaval in music is the result of the antagonism of Logos and Eros, or to put it another way, of Classicism versus Romanticism. Interestingly, this schism does not exist among primal peoples.

It is among contemporary Western artists and intellectuals who are attempting to reunify the intrinsic dualism of their cultures that we discover the most insightful descriptions of the ruptured mentality of the West as it contrasts with the holistic worldview of primal peoples. They see Plato as the purveyor of the Western disruption—though perhaps Aristotle was most responsible for axiomizing Platonic rationale. They believe that Plato's enthusiasm for a newfound Logos overwhelmed and decimated what Gilbert Murray called "the pre-Socratic cosmos of goddesses." Plato pointed out that Logos, by comparison to the obsolescent White Goddess mentality of the Greek dawn, was invariant, constant, harmonious, comprehensive, objective, reliable, and monopolistic insofar as it was universally true for all who grasped it. Therefore Plato characterized Logos not only as the ultimate good but also as *masculine*. On the other hand, Eros, which was the realm of the goddesses—relative, unreliable, subjective and aesthetic—was characterized by Plato as bad and *feminine*. Many twentieth-century intellectuals, including Northrop and Marcuse, believe that it is precisely this degradation of Eros which is responsible for the dehumanizing and devitalizing of Western society. Though all the arts may be envisioned as an emanation of what Plato would call Eros, it is dance and music in particular which have faced the most negative criticism during the history of the West, and traces of antimusic ideas can be found in Plato, Locke, Kant, Hegel, and then beyond them in the concepts of Goethe, Whitehead, Wittgenstein, and the Existentialists.

The most central issue in these philosophical rejections of music is based upon the inclination of Logos-bound minds to deprive music of any relationship with nature (sound). As Whitehead has pointed out, there is such a thing as "the fallacy of misplaced concreteness," which is the error of mistaking the abstract entities of thought for the concrete factors of reality itself. What this points up in terms of Western music is that there is a great deal of difference between what the ear is capable of hearing and what it wishes to hear. By excluding nature (sound) from music in the West the composer has been left only with Logos (reason) as the organizing basis for the work. Therefore the very essence of the musical conception is necessarily conditioned by the syntactical projections of language-bound Logos: dictating the structural causalities of A-B-A musical form, of harmonic limitations, or psychological purposes in music, and a tendency to compose music *about* things other than sound itself.

Western music reached its organizational limits toward the end of the nineteenth century when the Romanticism of Wagner, Mähler, Bruckner, Richard Strauss, and Schoenberg automatically overflowed into an Eros-oriented potential of non-Western music. It is crucial that we recognize in the ideas of Wagner a complex straining toward an alternative to Eros-bound Classicism: "When the *folk* invented melodies," he wrote in his discussion entitled *Opera and Drama:*

> it proceeded like the natural bodily person, who, by the exercise of sexual functions, begets and brings forth humanity. Civilized humanity, arriving at light of day, reveals itself at

once by its outer stature; not first by its hidden, inner organism. Greek art apprehended this humanity by its outer stature alone, and strove to mould a faithful, lifelike counterfeit.
Christianity, on the contrary, proceeded anatomically; it
wanted to find man's soul and so it opened and cut up his
body, and bared all that formless inner organism at which
our gaze rebelled, because it is not anything but organism
and is not soul. In searching for the soul, however, we had
slain the body; in hunting for the source of life we had destroyed life itself and all its utterances, arriving at nothing
but dead entrails. But the search for the *soul* is nothing more
or less than life itself; and what remains left over, for Christian anatomy to look upon, is only death. Thus it is that
Christianity choked the organic, visionary impulse of the
folk's life; it hacked into its flesh, and with its dualistic scis-
sors played havoc with even its artistic purity. The Tribe, in
which folk-people's artistic force can mount to full power,
finds itself alone with Nature and with its own kind, and
there alone these *folk* people are able to preserve the original
Folkslied, so indivorcibly ingrown with what civilization
longingly calls *poetry*.

Wagner's conclusion ideally restates, from the view of the
mid-nineteenth century, the quest for a visionary mentality
in the West:

In our civilization the vision of the *folk* has been sacrificed to
science. Just as poetry was constructed by the rules which
Aristotle abstracted from the tragic poets of Greece, so music
was dressed by scientific canons and assumptions. This was
at the time when even humanity was to be made by scholarly recipes, and from chemical concoctions. Mechanism was
to set up organism, or else to replace it entirely. But, in truth,
the restless mainspring of this mechanical inventiveness
drove ever toward the genuine visionary humanity. By
drawing upon mechanism rather than vision, we are put in
that chill of feelingless amazement which takes us when we
look upon a masterpiece of mere mechanism—a corpse or a
facsimile of life but never the living thing itself! Art of this

Western kind can only display a motionlessness that insists upon the momentum of a false concept of time. It can never make of the beholder a confident witness to the very becoming of a thing.

What we see happening in the work of Wagner and the other ultimate romanticists is the rules of Logos being overwhelmed by music itself—by sound as an emanation of nature rather than a projection of reason. In short, music recovered its primal relationship to the ear as a sensual, perceptive organ.

Among primal peoples, the natural world is not something alien and wild. It is not an enemy or an outside force that must be subdued and dominated. Nature is the aesthetic perfection with which we aspire to become identical, harmonious, and bound by immediacy and wholeness. It is therefore not surprising that among primal people music is the sound of the natural world made immediate and vivid by the perceptual miracle of the ear.

In such a primal scheme of sound, auditory space has no favored boundaries; it is an unfixed space shaped by the sound itself and not, as it is in the West, a space *containing* sounds. For the primal musician and singer (and for many contemporary Western composers who have learned directly and indirectly from tribal music) the space in which music exists is dynamic and relative, always in motion, creating its own dimensions from moment to moment. It has traditions and conventions, of course, but it does not fall faithfully into anything remotely like the classical A-B-A form of the West.

The impulse behind the creation of music is not expressional in the Western psychological sense but is brought into existence by a dynamic process which is inclusive rather than exclusive; which, so to speak, is natural rather than rational. Indians of the Americas are inspired by songs heard in visions and dreams. With this inspiration the singer produces music with absolute obedience to his or her inner impulse. Often the song which results is kept private and is never sung except in the mind of its creator; or it may be publicly performed and passed as a private possession to a beneficiary when its owner dies.

Originality is not an incentive among primal musicians any more than it was among the composers of the Middle Ages in the West, who commonly borrowed melodies from preexisting songs. "This was a widely practiced if little-known custom: of the 2542 surviving works of the troubadours of the Middle Ages, 514 are securely, and another 70 in all likelihood, reckoned to be imitations or borrowings with respect to their melodies. A fifth or more of this entire genre of music was 'unoriginal.' " (Francisco Navy, notes to *Cansos de Trobairitz; Stationen Europäischer Musik*, Cologne, 1978.) For the primal musician a song already in existence may be as much an inspiration as a song heard in the imagination or in a dream.

Since the Western conception of the privacy of the inner world in comparison to the public nature of the external world does not enter into the holistic way primal people think of consciousness and experience, there is no boundary between what is public and extant and what is formative and personal, at least not in the Western connotation. And just as primal music is not bound by the requirements of originality and public performance, so it is not bound by the limitations of duration and psychological purposes. Whereas Western music has a beginning, middle, and end and operates more or less vertically due to the uses of *accelerando* and *diminuendo, crescendo* and *decrescendo,* primal music is un-fixed in duration and development and operates horizontally insofar as it has relatively no psychological (emotional) preoccupations. Elements of these primal principles have recently surfaced in the experimental music of composers like Alan Hovhaness, Harry Partch, John Cage, Terry Riley, Philip Glass, and Steve Reich.

Western music is primarily melodic, consisting of temporal patterns of harmonic conventions drawn from a culture-bound tonal precept. Primal music may have purposes besides those of occupying the mind of the listener. It may address itself to the body and by a trancelike development provoke an ecstatic experience of mind and body which is rarely witnessed among Western listeners except in discos and Baptist churches.

When it is pointed out that *melody* is not central in most primal musical forms, it is often assumed that rhythm is therefore the only alternative core of non-Western music. But this is both an oversimplification and a misconception. The specific harmonic nature of what is meant by "melody" in the West is culturally predetermined by "what the ear wants to hear" and not by "what the ear is capable of hearing." Currently the precept of *melody* is as unacceptable to most contemporary Western composers as it is to many primal musicians. In discussing posttonal music in the West we have devised the term "line" as a means of avoiding the harmonic dogma implicit in the word *melody*. This contemporary Western term—*line*—has very much the same application to primal music as it does in contemporary posttonal music. It implies a *movement of tone* that is not formulated upon melodic structure—not the thirty-two–measure scheme so prevalent in tune-making and not the Western harmonic rules which reached their point of exhaustion during the late Romantic period in Europe (1880–1920). To the ear of the primal musician, what is important is not melody as we understand it in the West but the *entire sound* of music, its complete tonal and rhythmical reality. The totality of this musical experience touches the consciousness; not because of the magic of the words or the emotion of the music but because of the motion of the whole sound. For example, the mantra of Yoga and the dervish call are significant not because of their *meanings* but because of their *sounds*. It is the domination of Logos which has made us look for meaning in the music of the West, rather than listening for the immediacy of *sound itself*.

The music developed in North America by Indians is one of the world's distinctive musical idioms, for no other people made quite the same sounds even when they created similar instruments, such as drums, rattles, and whistles.

Besides the prevalence of drums and rattles, the most obvious characteristic of Indian music is the harshness of the vocal reproduction—a sort of flat, nonemotional sound that has certain parallels in the vocal music of the Near East. American Indian music is essentially unison vocal composition, performed with percussive accompaniment. Voice production is typically strong in accent, with tension in the vocal organs and an Asiaticlike pulsation on the long notes. It is music of a vertical or linear arrangement, in some ways not unlike the music of Java, Bali, and Japan. This kind of primal music does not excel in lavish harmonic embellishments and developments. The tonal line typically descends from higher to lower pitch in either terraced or downward cascading intervals that are very difficult for the Western ear to hear, since these intervals are, so to speak, the spaces *in between* the keys of the piano rather than the keys themselves—very much like the celebrated "blue notes" of Afro-American Blues. Therefore the tone of much primal music sounds "bent" to the European ear.

Melodic polyphony—the simultaneous voicing of two or more melodic lines—is nonexistent, except for an occasional drone-type accompaniment of a voice or voices using a single, sustained pitch, or the tradition by which women often sing in unison with the men but an octave higher. Instruments are used elaborately but are devoted solely to accompaniment; there being very little purely instrumental music, such as solo drumming or any other kind of instrumental virtuosity as we know it in Western music. Structurally, uneven bar lengths and asymmetrical rhythmic patterns are far more common than consistent measure lengths. As I have already indicated, the formalism of Logos-oriented structure (such as A-B-A form, etc.) is nonexistent in Native American music as well as in the music of most primal peoples.

American Indian music is not entirely limited to drums and rattles. Some tribes use wooden flutes, mostly for the music of courtship, and in the case of the Apache there is also a very basic stringed instrument called an Apache "fiddle" that is bowed and plucked. In recent years there has been an active revival of flute carving and playing among several tribes, even those that do not have a known history of flute music. The people of the Dakotas are excellent flutists and carve handsome instruments out of cedar and tie them with skin thongs. The Yaqui Indians of Northern Mexico (and Arizona) play Pacura flutes, and the Papago and Pima tribes of the Southwest have their own style of wind instruments which are used ceremonially.

The music of Indians is a literature of songs for various activities central to the life of the tribe and its people. There are, for instance, songs of healing which arise from the mystery of life and death. Numerous ceremonies are cycles of such curative songs concerned with restoring personal health as well as sustaining the fertility of crops and the abundance of game or the harmony of the whole tribe with the natural world. There are also individual songs that are highly prized and personal insofar as they often come out of lonely suffering and visionary trauma:

> It is only crying about myself
> That comes to me in song.   (NOOTKA)

Personal songs are also the embodiment of an acquired vision with great power for its fortunate owner. Apart from the curing songs, which usually possess fertility overtones, there are also songs exclusively concerned with growth and abundance, addressed to elements of nature and filled with marvelously keen observations:

> Blue evening falls
> Blue evening falls,
> Near by, in every direction,
> It sets the corn tassels trembling.   (PAPAGO)

Many Indian songs are ritualistic and serve as part of a greater activity than "music" as we understand it in the West. Many songs are descriptive in the special manner of Japanese Haiku—based upon a brilliantly direct and restrained aesthetic sensibility. Some of the songs are not "intelligible" as language, for they are derived from suggestive rather than explicit symbols. These songs contain texts based entirely or partially upon meaningless syllables. Texts may also include archaic words, loanwords, or even special phonemic alterations. These devices make the song text very different from the spoken prose style of a tribe and tend to obscure rather than enlighten the purpose behind the songs. Non-Indians tend to hear this restricted and special use of lyrics as primitive, while native people consider this procedure an important device of restraint and poetic ambiguity.

The American Indian world has a deep reverence for silence. Children are taught at a very early age to sit still and enjoy their solitude in the belief that from this quietude come the most elevated of creative experiences. The silence itself therefore becomes an aspect of the *total* sound of music. Only when we reach the compositions of Anton Webern do we discover a similar elevation of silence in Western music. From the solitude of Indians come songs of a special, highly personal nature evolved out of the consummate self—the self of open, calm privacy and centeredness. Such songs are not shared but kept strictly to oneself. Dream songs are also highly prized by Indians and, like songs of vision, come only to those who search for them. Fasting, long vigils, and sometimes the use of drugs such as jimsonweed are used to bring the song-bestowing dreams. Among the Plains tribes such songs are greatly valued as personal property, while among the Pueblo people a dream is likely to present a new song for the use of the whole community. As already noted, in a dream Wovoka was given the songs and dances of the Ghost Dance, which he passed on to all the tribes and which rapidly became the last, most desperate revivalist Indian ceremony in the 1890s.

There are also songs of death, which have a unique existence in Indian cultures, for they do not seem to exist for other peoples, so far as I can determine, with the single exception of the Japanese. The brave song—or death song—is a steadfast and eloquent expression of a person who confronts his or her own death. It is sung only at times of utter desolation or when the singer stands in the face of death itself. Other death songs are composed spontaneously at the very moment of death and are chanted with the last breath of the dying person.

> The odor of death,
> I smell the odor of death
> In front of my body.   (DAKOTA)

There is no aspect of the world that is not worthy of astonishment and which is not celebrated by Indians in music and rituals. That celebration is a depiction of the cumulative sensualism upon which the human psyche turns. It is a process that has reawakened in the best of serial and postserial music. In a letter of 1907 Alban Berg wrote, "At last we have realized that sensuality is not a weakness, not a surrendering to one's desires, but immense strength, the center of all our being and thought. Only through an understanding of the sensual, through a profound insight into the depths, or perhaps rather the heights, of mankind can one arrive at a true idea of the human psyche."

In the life-of-sound, the primal musician discovers the immediacy of the sensual world. This is equally true of the Balinese orchestra and the American Indian circle of drummers. Their music is the totality of numerous instruments, individually played but producing a unified contrapuntal tonal and rhythmical impact. Each player plays only one tonal line at a time. In the largest, most resonant instruments this line is only a simple phrase, slow and short and repeated again and again like an endless tape-loop. The smaller and higher-pitched instruments play in unison, performing tonal lines of exceedingly subtle and swiftly changing complexity. The combination of all of these "melodies" (which the Western ear does not hear as melodies but as modulating and redundant rhythms) produces a unique polyphony as well as a series of massive layers of sensual sound.

The fundamentality of primal music lies not in its originality or daring, its complexity of harmonic development, but in the intricate variations on the main themes and in the brilliant rhythmic complexities introduced by the lead drummer, who is the "conductor" of the orchestra and whose intricate gestures are a kind of choreographic form of conducting. This primal music is a superstructure of redundant 4/4 beats surrounding a creative core of exquisite syncopations and added beats, the improvised expression of the individual drummers. In primal music—of Africa, Oceania, Asia, and America—there is an outer composition, but there is also an inner pulsation, an inner core of the music's percussive and chordal life. What is often lacking in the music of Philip Glass, Steve Reich, and other Minimalist composers of the West is that essential inner core. Such Western composers have a complex lesson to learn from primal music— from which they borrow so much and so little. There is an inner and an outer music. When we are content with the outer shape of things and present them repeatedly as profound truth we are likely to be dealing with superficiality but calling it fundamentality.

When singer Nina Simone was about twelve years old she made this startlingly insightful notation in her diary: "All music is what awakes within us when we are reminded by the instruments; it is not the violins or the clarinets. It is not the beating of the drums—nor the score of the baritone singing his sweet romanza; nor that of the men's chorus, nor that of the women's chorus. It is nearer and farther than they."

8

IDENTITY

Whether it happened so or not I do not know; but if you think about it you can see that it is true.

—BLACK ELK

We are what we pretend to be, so we must be careful about what we pretend to be.

—KURT VONNEGUT, JR.

We are what we imagine. Our very existence consists in our imagination of ourselves. . . . The greatest tragedy that can befall us is to go unimagined.

—N. SCOTT MOMADAY (1966)

From the Native American perspective the most fearsome dogma of Western reality is probably the fact that personal identity is both absolute and final at the same time that it is unavoidably public. It is inconceivable to the traditional Indian that *the self* is not allowed to exist in the West unless it is willing to be on perpetual public display. Indians find it incredible that a person must retain one identity, one name, one persona for his or her entire existence, no matter what immense changes may take place in that person's life. These contrasting attitudes about personal realities and the place of *the self* in the group make it clear that there are great differences between the way Indians and people of the West regard identity.

TRIBAL BEING

Vine Deloria, Jr. (1973) provided a keen insight into the most fundamental aspect of tribalism among Native Americans when he wrote that "there is no salvation in tribal religions apart from the continuance of the tribe itself." The implicit homogeneity of tribal mentality means that there can be no deviations from collective doctrine simply because there is no need for doctrine in a society in which there are numerous taboos but virtually no heresies. As a whole, Indian religions do not conceive of a personal relationship between sacred power (what would be called deity in the West) and each individual person. "It is rather," as Deloria notes, "a covenant between a particular god and a particular community."

This does not mean that the "individual" is nonexistent among Indian communities nor that each person cannot possess an access to sacredness; but it does mean that the highly individuated egocentricity of the Western soul is alien to Indians. The reality of persona is not preempted by the existence of communal homogeneity; but being a person and being an individual, in the Western sense of that term, are quite different experiences. Only in the West are the concepts of personality and individuality congruent. Thus the peoples of various cultures do not simply see events and objects differently from one another, but they also understand themselves as persons in quite different ways.

Primal cultures tend to be tribal rather than idiosyncratic in their psychology. For instance, most North American tribes possess what must be called a "communal soul" in comparison with the Western precept of the soul as personal property that ensures, under certain moral regulations, the eternal perpetuation of the private ego. Among the Iroquoian people the power that vivifies the tribe is called *orenda*; and it is this force which briefly animates the members of the tribe. People enrich or enervate the power that gives them life, and then they pass out of existence (since there is exceedingly little emphasis in North America upon anything approximating the afterlife of Christianity). What remains is the tribe; the community; the *orenda*.

The ego orientation and social narcissism of the West, along with the popular elaborations of a show-stopping entity called the *psyche*, are almost inconceivable to the primal populations of the world, which invest very little importance in every machination, twist, and turn of the private person. And though the West, which dotes on its Hellenic heritage of high-minded individualism, believes that it invented the notion of the *private person* at the dawn of history, the fact remains that individuality as it is now understood is a concept of very recent vintage. A tacit recognition of the relative novelty of individualism in the West helps us to understand that the conception of personality among primal peoples was until recently very closely parallel to the Western view of persona.

It was in America that individualism was born. The U.S.A. quickly became the symbol to Europeans of what liberal democracy would be in the entire world. Alexis de Tocqueville expounded upon this European view of America in his famous analysis of the 1830s. To depict the effects of American liberalism on the population of the United States, Tocqueville employed the French word *individualism,* and the term was thus introduced into the English language through the translation of Tocqueville's *Democracy in America.*

Americans had long prided themselves upon their sense of independence and personal identity without having a word for it, and so Tocqueville's term was introduced at an ideal time. In the decades before the Civil War romantic connotations of dynamism and ambitiousness infused new meaning into the concept of the free individual, different from what the republican founding fathers of the U.S.A. had understood or meant by "personal freedom." Now individuals were capable of far more than uncoerced options to have freedom; they also had to have the opportunity to develop their natural talents. Equal opportunity became a significant condition of individualism as it was understood in America; and of all the accesses to equality the most valued was education. It was education, however, of a very special kind; for it envisioned that barbarism and all the other deviations that separated peoples could and should be obliterated by knowledge. Thus, it became mandatory to be an educated individual; and all good Americans were expected to take advantage of their opportunities to become the same as everyone else and therefore as good as everybody else. If every American did not become a success it was clearly the individual's own fault.

The romantic American scheme of individualism lost much of its validity as it was tested by the realities of sexual, racial, and class distinctions, and as it gave way to the consensus that some people are more equal than others. The success of the individual has not been judged by the intentions or aspirations of people themselves but by social standards of success which are every bit as devastating and alienating to the individual as the mandates of behavior in nations which do not celebrate freedom and individualism.

"The possibility of conceiving of an individual alone in a tribal religious sense is ridiculous," Deloria (1970) has written. "The very complexity of tribal life and the interdependence of people on one another makes this conception improbable at best, a terrifying loss of identity at worst." In other words, the Western (American) connotation of individualism does not work in societies in which interdependence is a substantial and experiential reality rather than a political slogan. In tribal religions there is no salvation apart from the continuance of the tribe itself because the existence of the individual presupposes the existence of the community. Every element of tribal experience is necessarily understood as part of the largest meaning of life insofar as life (*orenda*) does not exist without the tribe which gives animation to its members. Yet the deviations of the individual are taken for granted because each person is part of the whole.

It is through relationships that Native Americans comprehend themselves. Such relationships are richly orchestrated, as we have already seen, by elaborations of languages and ritual activities. Underlying the identity of the tribe and the experience of personality in the individual is the sacred sense of place that provides the whole group with its centeredness. The Indian individual is spiritually interdependent upon the language, folk history, ritualism, and geographical sacredness of his or her *whole* people. Relationships between members of families, bands, clans, and other tribal groups are defined and intensified through relational and generational language rather than through personal names, which are considered to be sacred and private to the individual. The relatedness of the individual and the tribe extends outward beyond the family, band, or clan to include all things of the world. Thus nothing exists in isolation. Individualism does not presuppose autonomy, alienation, or isolation. And freedom is not the right to express yourself but the far more fundamental right to *be* yourself.

The image that grows out of the depiction of tribal identity is a startling form of individualism unknown in the West except within the underground of artists and various social and sexual deviants. For the abiding principle of tribalism is the vision of both nature and a society which provides a place for absolutely everything and everyone. "One could say," Deloria (1973) notes in his discussion of human personality, "that the tribal religions created the tribal community, which, in turn, made a place for every tribal individual. Christianity, on the other hand, appears to have created the solitary individual who, gathered together every seven days, constitutes the 'church,' which then defines the extent to which the religion is to be understood and followed."

TRIBAL INDIVIDUALITY

One of the most significant features of Indian tribal custom is the giving of individuated names. Such Indian names denote personal qualities, heroic exploits, uncommon abilities, unique physical characteristics, visionary experiences, and other designations that point specifically to the singularity of the person being named. Almost without exception every North American Indian is given, in a tribal ceremony, a name that recognizes his uniqueness.

The way in which names are given in the contemporary Western world has not only a different result but also an entirely different aim. The name George Washington, for instance, is not a personal name in the Indian sense. To the contrary, as Deloria points out, it indicates that for an undetermined number of generations the male member of the genetic line has been called Washington. It also indicates that the first president's parents were fond of the name George or had a prior relative whom they wished to honor by naming their child after him. A name like George Washington hardly indicates a unique and personal self; what it does is denote a genetic line. It is also a statistical reality to such an extent that the name given at birth is usually referred to as that person's "real" name. What accumulates around that statistical appointment, besides reputation, are various economic and historical data that are part of the public record: social security number, passport number, date of birth, annual income, and similar elements of what, in the West, are regarded as factual information. But such facts do not inform us about the person in the way that the Indian naming of an individual informs us.

It is significant that in the West names are fixed and public while among primal societies names are often changed by the tribe throughout a person's life, and such names are personal and, perhaps, private. In the West we are committed like prisoners to our public identities, to our sex and our age and our race. And no one will permit us to escape the statistical barriers used to name and to define us. But for most primal peoples there are a vast number of options available in terms of both who they are and what kind of world they wish to inhabit. Since primal society is inclusive rather than exclusive, since it recognizes everything in nature as natural, there is therefore an appropriate place for all behavior within the tribal structure—though many forms of behavior might be considered peculiar and perhaps undesirable to other societies. Not only does a primal person have a variety of ways by which he or she may fit into the social structure, but people also have a very wide potentiality for changing themselves and their identities even after they have been defined by social circumstances and roles.

Not only are primal people permitted to change their names, but since names are sacred designations of being, people also have the ability to be transformed—briefly or permanently—into other beings and animals. They are often permitted to change their gender, and they will be greatly admired for what would be considered personal peculiarities in the West.

The sacred clown and his apparently antisocial behavior which is condoned in Indian ceremonies seems outrageous to Western people who believe it is savage for a culture to institutionalize behavior that seems to be psychotic and perverted. "Many people who know about these things say that the clown is the most powerful," an Apache has commented when asked about the comic role of the sacred clown in ceremonies. "People think that the clown is just nothing, that he is just for fun. That is not so."

The clown exists in almost every Indian culture of North America. The Dakota (Sioux) clown is called *heyoka,* a person who has been given the greatest possible vision, that of the Thunder Being. After this experience the Thunder Being "wears" the *heyoka* in a manner not unlike the way a holy man wears a sacred object around his neck. While worn by the Thunder Being, a new *heyoka* reverses his behavior, speaking contrarily, riding backward on his horse, and doing everything in the opposite manner from his normal behavior. People look upon the *heyoka* with amusement and respect, for he represents a duplexity which Indians grasp as fundamental to life. The extraordinary is generally condemned and loathed by deeply traditional people, but Indians regard the extraordinary person as special and awesome, gifted and sacred. They accept perversity as a significant reality. Among Western people the "freak" is a pitiful target of ridicule—the perfect embodiment of the disdain for oddity and the inclination to regard peculiarity as irrationality and deformity as punishment for sin. The Indian, as Lame Deer perfectly expressed it, has a far more diversified metaphysical viewpoint: "Fooling around, the clown is really performing a spiritual ceremony." The clown's behavior is a vivification of his knowledge of *another* reality.

Clowns possess complete liberty, from the contrariness of the Cheyenne to the *neweekwe* clowns of the Zuñi. Their targets of ridicule are themselves as well as others. They also turn their metaphysical comedy upon shamans and other high religious authorities. The Navajo clown participates in the Mountain Chant by burlesquing the sacred sleight-of-hand tricks of the ceremony, revealing their secrets and disrupting the ritual with laughter and nonsense. A parallel to such mordant antics may be seen in the Theatre of the Absurd, where we discover in the characters of Samuel Beckett and Eugene Ionesco people for whom the bizarre, the irrational, the comic, and the tragic are utterly compatible. The plays of the Absurd dramatize the horror of metaphysical ir-rationality in grotesque dialogue and actions—a rather apt description of at least some aspects of the performances of sacred clowns. The disruptive antics of the clowns force peo-ple to look at things twice—first, seeing the apparent acts of religious life, and then, seeing the ineffable power behind the ceremonial surface.

This disrespect for mythic genuineness is an essential ele-ment of primal mentality, for it forces the initiated to accept the reality that lies behind appearances. Surely this insis-tence upon the reality of essences (rather than the belief in appearances) is the motive behind the Hopi initiation of their children. When adolescents are initiated into their clans they are permitted for the first time to witness the un-masking of the kachina impersonators. This seemingly bru-tal experience represents the gateway to a marvelous reality that cannot be shattered by the Western conception of verisi-militude.

In the autobiography of a Hopi Indian, *Sun Chief* (Sim-mons), the initiation is described in detail: "When the ka-chinas entered the kiva without masks, I had a great sur-prise. They were not spirits, but human beings. I recognized nearly every one of them and felt very unhappy, because I had been told all my life that the kachinas were gods. I was especially shocked and angry when I saw all my uncles, fa-thers, and clan brothers dancing as kachinas."

It is easy to interpret these events as devastating from the Western viewpoint, but it seems to me that the Indian van-tage suggests a heightening of spirituality rather than the opposite. Once the shock has turned into recognition the ini-tiate has acquired a mature and marvelous grasp of reality. It is perhaps a bit similar to our experience in art. When we are deeply moved by a painting we believe in its genuineness as a physical fact. But when we move closer to it and realize that it is composed of canvas and paint its reality is not destroyed for us—because the reality of art does not depend upon substantiality. The real power of both kachinas and paintings comes from their ability to transform one thing into another, to contain many realities rather than representing a single set of statistical elements that appear real to us.

Clowns vivify the widest possible vision of reality by showing us human nature in all of its manifestations. In 1882 Adolph Bandelier visited Chochiti Pueblo in New Mexico and made outraged notes: "The whole is a filthy, obscene affair. They were drinking urine out of bowls and jars used as privies on the house tops, eating excrements and dirt." Sexuality is a favored subject of clowns, perhaps because it is an area in which humanity is vulnerable. They talk, sing, and joke about it constantly. They enact sexual displays that would be shocking in other societies and that would be equally unusual, I might add, among the normally modest Indian tribes were it not for the special liberty granted clowns. Before the missionaries descended upon the Southwest, the Pueblo clowns wore enormous dildos and often exhibited themselves. Bandelier's diary of 1880 expresses his shock when witnessing a Cochiti ceremony: "They chased after her, carried her back and threw her down in the center of the plaza, then while one was performing the coitus from behind, another was doing it against her head. Of course, all was simulated, and not the real act, as the woman was dressed. The naked fellow performed masturbation in the center of the plaza or very near it, alternately with a black rug and his hand. Everybody laughed."

The report of Bandelier expressed shock and dismay, a response of many ethnologists who, despite their repulsion, fortunately recorded these clown rites in the era prior to their total repression (c. 1920) by the Bureau of Indian Affairs and Protestant missionaries. There was also a period when art critics were perplexed by the raw sexuality of novels and films in their own societies; in fact, a preoccupation with criticism of obscenity has been so distracting that most critics missed the philosophical and artistic achievements of writers like James Joyce and D. H. Lawrence. Today, however, the concept of sexuality as a vital, expressive vehicle for nonsexual ideas is no longer peculiar or strange to Western society. Post-Freudian ideas about sex have extended into politics and metaphysics, assuming a metaphoric vitality that makes possible the expression of themes and values previously inaccessible to the West. The American Indians' sacred clown has for centuries epitomized the vitality of perversity, humor, sexuality, aggressiveness, and absurdity—a mentality possible only for those beyond duality and dichotomies of flesh and spirit, sacred and profane, individual and tribal.

It is quite impossible to explain Indian ceremonial reality except by pointing up similar behavior in Western society which, though taken entirely for granted, is exceedingly peculiar from the primal point of view. Take for example the institutionalization of the behavior of people who give full vent to their inclination to speak other people's words and to perform other people's actions as if they were their own. If this kind of "make-believe" is not strange enough, add to the situation the fact that these impersonators are highly paid professionals who claim to be schooled in their strange imitations of other people, and whose excellence in their perverse game is recognized by veritable public worship. These experts are called *actors*. Their role in society is completely taken for granted in the West, but among primal peoples it is inconceivable for such performers to exist outside the priesthood or the ritual groups that perform sacred ceremonies.

The institutionalization of other kinds of performances by the West is equally peculiar to primal peoples. For instance, to Eskimos who did not have jails or policemen for centuries, how could one possibly explain the fact that some societies train and pay men to chase, shoot, capture, and cage people?

And for many primal people for whom capital punishment is simply inconceivable, how would one explain the fact that great nations train and pay a special elite of killers who chop off people's heads, hang them, or strap them into chairs and either send thousands of volts of electricity into their bodies or suffocate them with deadly gas?

The stereotypes of individuals in the society of the dominant culture are so much taken for granted that it is extremely difficult to realize how differently other people see themselves in relation to one another. As the policeman and the executioner represent authority in the stark reality of the West, the sacred clown represents authority in the metaphoric world of primal society. The clown ritualizes and stabilizes human behavior on the same ceremonial stage where Western actors, deprived centuries ago of their power to instruct, are now viewed simply as entertainers.

In a very important way the clown also represents the birth of the idiosyncratic—or, as Western people would probably see it, the birth of the individual. Normally the *orenda*—the tribal power—is essentially a group "soul" that is manifested in each baby as it is initiated into the tribe and that carries a person through life. The sacred clown, however, appears to alter this unity of the tribal relationship to the communal and nonindividual power of the *orenda*. Usually the members of the tribe are not special, their power is not essentially individual in the Western sense, nor does it possess any public individuating characteristics. Their "souls" are community property, especially among the tribes of the Southwest, which are very conservative and extremely conformist—the "individual" has little value to the Southwestern Indian society. The Plains tribes, on the other hand, are involved in vision quests that are quite individualized, resulting in visions that are both personal and powerful.

But regardless of this "individuality," there is nothing in Indian tribal life that even begins to approximate the Western conception of individuality and free will. It follows that Indian societies do not provide a place for "individuals" and therefore such societies do not provide regulations that govern the limits of individuality. Whites are extremely devoted to limiting the rights of individuals and preventing anarchy, which is greatly feared by highly individualized cultures. By contrast the Indian, generally speaking, does not recognize the individual and therefore has not formulated strict regulations for his control. The thrust of the ego in the individual is so slight a threat to the public life of Indian tribes that common gossip and ceremonialized ridicule are sufficient to keep people living together harmoniously. There were no jails in pre-Columbian North America. Only occasionally was it necessary to cast out a member of the tribe—an act similar in effect to the death sentence in other cultures. Because individualism was viewed from an entirely different standpoint by Indians than it was by Europeans, idiosyncratic behavior, perversity, and actions that were highly deviant and nonconformist were not looked upon as a demonstration of madness, or as the threat of anarchy, or as the expression of heresy. Such behavior was seen by Indians as a manifestation of great power and spirituality and regarded with considerable respect. The clowns were permitted to be exceptional. Anyone in the tribe who was perverse was automatically provided with a significant rather than a degraded role in society.

As a group the clowns represent the rise of a unique sort of individuality in ancient Indian cultures, possessing the extraordinary power, the privilege, the license, and the expressive freedom denied everyone else. As we witness the role assigned to clowns in ceremonies and in tribal life generally, we see clearly the way in which they assume a function for Indians similar, perhaps, to the saints, the prophets, and especially the artists of the Western world; they are those whose specialness provides a human connection between the accessible and the inaccessible. Ultimately these outsiders, these glorious clowns and contraries, symbolize the act of initiation that raises us from the commonplace and gives us access to the extraordinary. As the people of Acoma Pueblo say of their first clown: "He knew something about himself."

TRANSFORMATIONS

Almost none of the alternative identities available to Indians are accessible to the people of the West. With the exception of the religious transformations of Catholic initiates and women who change their names, family ties, and loyalties when they are married, no personal transformations are acceptable in the West. I am reminded of *Arsenic and Old Lace* by Russel Crouse and Howard Lindsay in which a character thinks he's Teddy Roosevelt. Someone asks his sister: "Have you ever tried to tell him he isn't Teddy Roosevelt?" and she answers: "Once we tried to suggest that he was George Washington and he just laid under his bed and wouldn't be anybody."

We appear to be in search of alternative identities in our disillusioned society and yet a good many of us are unwilling to be anybody. In one of the Don Juan books of Carlos Castaneda, the young Carlos's automobile vanishes and reappears. Stupefied, Carlos asks Don Juan and Don Gregorio if his car had *really* disappeared. The Yaqui holy men laugh and reply that "everything *really* happens." I've quoted that scene by Castaneda in a previous chapter, but it bears repetition here because it is a very powerful metaphor about the primal mind. Yet it is difficult to find many readers of Castaneda who are not inclined to ask if the tales of Don Juan *really* happened—if they are fact or fiction. Of course, these readers have entirely missed the point—since the importance of Castaneda's books has nothing whatever to do with such a naive question.

What is most devastating is that not only skeptics ask this question but also people seriously searching for some alternatives to their society's realism. They apparently want to discover a source of power and inspiration that will help them escape the materialism of their own world, but what they really hope to find is some kind of science fiction that duplicates their accustomed materialism but does so with a dash of mystery and mysticism: with tales of Atlantis, Mu, and god-astronauts from outer space who brought culture to the earth in their astral chariots. They do not really want revelation but a cosmetic transformation of their own bankrupt world into Disneyland. So they still ask if Castaneda's books are fictive because they are still stuck with an outdated realism despite their intense dissatisfaction with it.

Their resistance to transformation includes their inability to accept the changing identities of other people. When a drastic change is undertaken in their society, like the surgical alteration of gender, they insist, unless ignorant of the operation, upon retaining the old identity of the person and never willingly or fully accept what is apparently a desperate effort to alter social reality. People who are uncomfortable with their given names and change them constantly are called by their "real" names in their absence. People who devotedly change religions are never fully accepted in the faith of their choice. Identity is a prison in the West. Yet, among primal peoples, there are numerous societal and personal ceremonies that make all types of drastic changes in identity and reality possible for virtually everyone. And these changes are considered actual transformations.

Anthropologist Matilda Coxe Stevenson, in a report on the Zuñi Indians, based on fieldwork dating to 1896–97, movingly described the death of her friend We'wha, a Zuñi male transvestite, whose original gender had been unknown to Stevenson, and apparently unknown to President Cleveland and other politicians whom We'wha had visited during a six-month stay in Washington, D.C. (I am quoting Dr. Stevenson at length because I feel that her narration clarifies in experiential terms the way in which the Native American individual relates to tribal identity.)

A death which caused universal regret and distress in Zuñi was that of We'wha, undoubtedly the most remarkable member of the tribe. This person was a man wearing woman's dress, and so carefully was his sex concealed that for years the writer believed him to be a woman. Some declared him to be an hermaphrodite, but the writer gave no credence to the story, and continued to regard We'wha as a woman; and as he was always referred to by the tribe as "she"—it being their custom to speak of men who don woman's dress as if they were women—and as the writer could never think of her faithful and devoted friend in any other light, she will continue to use the feminine gender when referring to We-'wha. She was perhaps the tallest person in Zuñi: certainly the strongest, both mentally and physically. Her skin was much like that of the Chinese in color, many of the Zuñis having this complexion. During six months' stay in Washington she became several shades lighter. She had a good memory, not only for the lore of her people, but for all that she heard of the outside world. She spoke only a few words of English before coming to Washington, but acquired the language with remarkable rapidity, and was soon able to join in conversation. She possessed an indomitable will and an insatiable thirst for knowledge. Her likes and dislikes were intense. She would risk anything to serve those she loved, but toward those who crossed her path she was vindictive. Though severe she was considered just. At an early age she lost her parents and was adopted by a sister of her father. She belonged to the Badger clan, her foster mother belonging to the Dogwood clan. Owing to her bright mind and excellent memory, she was called upon by her own clan and also by the clans of her foster mother and father when a long prayer had to be repeated or a grace was to be offered over a feast. In fact she was the chief personage on many occasions. On account of her physical strength all the household work requiring great exertion was left for her, and while she most willingly took the harder work from others of the family, she would not permit idleness; all had to labor or receive an upbraiding from We'wha, and nothing was more dreaded than a scolding from her.

In the fall of 1896 a Sha'läko god was entertained at her home. Although at this time We'wha was suffering from valvular heart disease, she did most of the work, including the laying of a stone floor in the large room where the ceremonial was to occur. She labored early and late so hard that when the time came for holding the ceremony she was unable to be present. From this time she was listless and remained alone as much as possible, though she made no complaint of illness. When a week or more had passed after the close of the great autumn ceremonial of the Sha'läko, and the many guests had departed, the writer dropped in at sunset to the spacious room in the house of We'wha's foster father, the late José Palle. We'wha was found crouching on the ledge by the fireplace. That a great change had come over her was at once apparent. Death evidently was rapidly approaching. She had done her last work. Only a few days before this strong-minded, generous-hearted creature had labored to make bread for the reception of her gods; now she was preparing to go to her beloved Ko'thluwala'wa. When the writer asked, "Why do you not lie down?" We'wha replied: "I can not breathe if I lie down: I think my heart break." The writer at once sent to her camp for a comfortable chair, and fixed it at a suitable angle for the invalid, who was most grateful for the attention. There was little to be done for the sufferer. She knew that she was soon to die and begged the writer not to leave her.

From the moment her family realized that We'wha was in a serious condition they remained with her, ever ready to be of assistance. The family consisted of the aged foster mother, a foster brother, two foster sisters with their husbands and children, and her own brother with his wife and children. The writer never before observed such attention as every member of the family showed her. The little children ceased their play and stood in silence close to their mothers, occasionally toddling across the floor to beg We'wha to speak. She smiled upon them and whispered, "I can not talk." The foster brother was as devoted as the one related by blood.

During two days the family hoped against hope. Nai'uchi, the great theurgist, came three times and pretended to draw from the region of the heart bits of mutton, declared to have been "shot" there by a witch who was angry with We'wha for not giving her a quarter of mutton when she asked for it. We'wha appeared relieved when the theurgist left. She knew that she was dying and appeared to desire quiet. After Nai'uchi's last visit, the foster brother, with streaming eyes, prepared te'likinawe (prayer plumes) for the dying, the theurgist having said that her moments on earth were few. We'wha asked the writer to come close and in a feeble voice she said, in English: "Mother, I am going to the other world. I will tell the gods of you and Captain Stevenson. I will tell them of Captain Carlisle, the great seed priest, and his wife, whom I love. They are my friends.* Tell them good-by. Tell all my friends in Washington good-by. Tell President Cleveland, my friend, good-by. Mother, love all my people; protect them; they are your children; you are their mother." These sentences were spoken with many breaks. The family seemed somewhat grieved that We'wha's last words should be given to the writer, but she understood that the thoughts of the dying were with and for her own people. A good-by was said to the others, and she asked for more light.

It is the custom for a member of the family to hold the prayer plumes near the mouth of the dying and repeat the prayer, but this practice was not observed in We'wha's case.

*At the time of We'wha's visit to Washington the Hon. John G. Carlisle was Speaker of the House of Representatives. The Speaker and Mrs. Carlisle were very kind to We'wha, and upon her return to Zuñi she found a great sack of seed which had been sent by the Speaker.

She requested the writer to raise the back of the chair, and when this was done she asked if her prayer plumes had been made. Her foster brother answered "Yes," whereupon she requested him to bring them. The family suppressed their sobs that the dying might not be made sad. The brother offered to hold the plumes and say the prayers, but We'wha feebly extended her hand for them, and clasping the prayer plumes between her hands made a great effort to speak. She said but a few words and then sank back in her chair. Again the brother offered to hold the plumes and pray, but once more she refused. Her face was radiant in the belief that she was going to her gods. She leaned forward with the plumes tightly clasped, and as the setting sun lighted up the western windows, darkness and desolation entered the hearts of the mourners, for We'wha was dead.

Blankets were spread upon the floor and the brothers gently laid the lifeless form upon them. After the body was bathed and rubbed with meal, a pair of white cotton trousers were drawn over the legs, the first male attire she had worn since she had adopted woman's dress years ago. The rest of her dress was female. The body was dressed in the finest clothing; six shawls of foreign manufacture, gifts from Washington friends, besides her native blanket wraps, and a white Hopi blanket bordered in red and blue, were wrapped around her. The hair was done up with the greatest care. Three silver necklaces, with turquoise earrings attached and numerous bangles, constituted the jewels.

We'wha's death was regarded as a calamity, and the remains lay in state for an hour or more, during which time not only members of the clans to which she was allied, but the rain priests and theurgists and many others, including children, viewed them. When the blanket was finally closed, a fresh outburst of grief was heard, and then all endeavored to suppress their sobs, for the aged foster mother had fallen unconscious to the floor. The two brothers carried the remains unattended to the grave. The sisters made food offerings to the fire. The foster brother on his return prepared prayer plumes for each member of the immediate family, and also the writer. The little procession, including the foster mother, who had recovered sufficiently to accompany the others, then made its way to the west of the village and on the river bank deposited the clothing, mask, and prayer plumes in the manner heretofore described. Upon the return to the house the foster mother had the rest of We'wha's possessions brought together that they might be destroyed. All her cherished gifts from Washington friends, including many photographs, were brought out; all must be destroyed. This work was performed by the mother, who wept continually. All was sacrificed but pictures of Mr. and Mrs. Carlisle, Mr. Stevenson, and the writer. These were left in their frames on the wall. With another outburst of grief the old woman declared they must remain, saying: "We'wha will have so much with her. I can not part with these. I must keep the faces of those who loved We'wha and whom she loved best. I must keep them to look upon."

WE ARE ALL RELATED

There is great variety in Native American personality just as there is considerable diversity in the cultures of Indians. In an informal social situation, for example, the white person may become progressively more talkative, while some traditional, older Indians may stand quietly saying or doing nothing, monitoring the other rather than themselves for cues regarding the adequacy of that one's responses. If addressed directly the Indian may not look at the speaker since such directness may be considered aggressive. There may be delay before the reply. For some Indian students, to be singled out in praise is a source of shame; for others, to look directly into the eyes of another person is an act of rudeness. Yet other Indians may be capable of social niceties, of joking and robust conversation. Clearly Indians are regionally, tribally, and personally different from one another, and my efforts to focus upon overriding elements of aborginal temperament and lifestyle should not reinforce the stereotypical notions of Indians any more than a generalized perspective of European history should suggest that the highly divergent peoples of England, Bulgaria, Norway, and Portugal are identical to one another.

Harold E. Driver has summarized contemporary ethnological insights into Native American personality, giving attention to the generalizations of observers at the same time that he has made it clear that each observer has tended to find whatever he wished to find in a studied culture, and one set of documented tribal traits therefore tends to contradict the traits noted by other experts. The case of the Pueblo Indians is the most famous of such contradictions: "The four descriptions of Pueblo personality, all published within a span of twelve years, clearly fall into two groups: the Benedict-Thompson Apollonian ideal; the Eggan-Goldfrank maladjusted actuality." Two independent observers found the Puebloan peoples to be ideally peaceful and adjusted while two other observers depicted them as highly neurotic and repressed by social pressures.

Though there is unquestionable value in the specialized depiction by outsiders of the personal temperament of aboriginal peoples, it is probable that for our purposes the insights of generalists such as Joseph Epes Brown are more to the point, since they speak metaphorically and thus allow the act of observation to have an experiential impact that draws us *into* an alien existence rather than, consciously or unconsciously, drawing tenuous parallels between ourselves and others. "All forms under creation," Epes Brown writes, "were understood to be mysteriously interrelated. Everything was as a relative to every other being or 'thing.' Thus, nothing existed in isolation. The intricately interrelated threads of the spider's web [were thought] to depict the world. The same reference occurs in native American art. This is a profound 'symbol,' when it is understood. The people obviously observed that the threads of the web were drawn out from within the spider's very being. They also recognized that the threads in concentric circles were sticky whereas the threads leading to the center were smooth!"

One vivid expression of the tribal sense of centeredness is perfectly expressed in the Plains Indian ceremonies involving communal smoking. At the conclusion of the pipe ceremony the participants murmur: "We are all related." The act of smoking is a ritual of communion with *everything* in creation, with every possibility of being—what lies before us and also what lies beyond our understanding and knowledge. "We are all related." In the Native American experience, all things are possible and therefore all things are acceptable. R. D. Laing explains that "when we destroy a people's experience they become destructive." It is desirable, then, for our societal structures to be bold and large enough to affirm rather than to deny. The tribal relationship of Indians is therefore never based upon the tolerance of others, but the experience of the self as part of others. *"We are all related."*

III

THE FUTURE
OF THE PRIMAL
MIND

9

ALIENATION
AS METAPHOR

> [The poet possesses] the feeling for syllable and rhythm, pen-
> etrating far below the conscious levels of thought and feel-
> ing, invigorating every word; sinking to the most primitive
> and forgotten, returning to the origin and bringing some-
> thing back, seeking the beginning and the end. It works
> through meanings, certainly, or not without meanings in the
> ordinary sense, and fuses the old and obliterated and trite,
> the current and the new and surprising, the most ancient and
> the most civilized mentality.
>
> —T. S. ELIOT

In all spheres of Indian life *harmony*, as we have seen, was
mandatory—a condition of nature itself, the resonance of a
kind of *sanity* that predates psychology. The turbulence and
velocity of change in the West which has epitomized the
destiny of the nineteenth and twentieth centuries was unknown among Indians. Such drastic change—revolutionary,
internal change—was not typical of the lives of tribal peoples who did not produce an Einstein, Freud, Darwin, or Picasso to disrupt and fundamentally alter their worldview.
The invention of agriculture in America, the reintroduction
of the horse to this hemisphere—these were forces that
caused great, pervasive changes in the lives of Indians, but
these were not the kinds of internal, individualized convic-
tions that challenge the cultural status quo. Such rebelliousness is unheard of among primal peoples, who have an ex-

quisite homogeneity that puts them directly in touch with their culture and with its prescribed and perpetuated forms.

When Alfred North Whitehead delivered his famous words about the future he was speaking to scholars of the West and had no idea that his observations might one day awaken in primal people a sense of daring. "It is the business of the future to be dangerous," he said. "The major advances in civilization are processes that all but wreck the societies in which they occur."

In the decade when Whitehead uttered those prophetic phrases the Native American was fighting brilliantly to retain the past that missionaries and government teachers were attempting to obliterate. Those tenacious Indians of the 1920s were not reaching for the future but striving for an identity almost stolen away from them. In all spheres of Native American life harmony within the tribe was a defense against alienation. Even culturally, the highly individuated concept that brings about the artist and his or her idiosyncratic efforts to achieve expressive originality was virtually unknown among Indians and other aboriginal craftspeople, whose work was considered to be no more rarefied or specialized than the work of the farmer, shaman, hunter, or any other person of the tribe.

But this communal conformity was never limited strictly to primal peoples. Even in the West, rebelliousness and intellectual and artistic inventiveness were relatively new and radical precepts which we now take for granted. Europeans of the time of Columbus had a very dim view of heretics and only recently learned how to live with and even profit from their creative anarchy. The Romantic Age, with its emphasis upon personal experiences, feelings, and visions, greatly implemented the recognition of a professional person such as the artist. Today we take it for granted that Western people have always celebrated such superstar iconoclasts as Pablo Picasso, but as art historian Herbert Read has shown, "the self" in art and in daily life is an invention of fairly recent times. "Even when in later historical times," Read (1966) wrote, "the artist was differentiated from other craftsmen, and his skill was developed as an individual talent, when then there was the strongest impulse to achieve an ideal uniformity, and although distinct personalities do emerge among the sculptors, for instance, of classical Greece, it is very difficult to ascribe any personal accents to the work of a Myron or a Praxiteles—they did not express, and were not expected to express, *the uniqueness of an individuality.*" Only gradually did the West invent the individual. But among primal people such an expression of the self is still not acceptable, to such an extent that originality is generally looked upon as a fault.

In the 1920s, about the time that Whitehead formulated his disquieting description of the future, the Zia Indian painter Velino Herrera (Mé Pe Wi) was accused by his tribe of providing drawings of the sacred sun symbol of his Puebloan people to officials of the State of New Mexico, who subsequently adapted it as their circular logo. Herrera's behavior was considered so outrageously individualistic, even for Indians of the early twentieth century, that he was cast out by his people, his property was confiscated, and he never again won reacceptance by his tribe. His "error" was not simply a matter of allegedly giving away secrets to the white man; his fundamental "crime" was the fact that he acted out of personal conviction. His actions betrayed whatever it is within us that we call *ourselves.*

It is taboo among primal people like Indians for someone to depart from communal mentality. Traditional Indians reject this kind of behavior as antisocial and treasonous; and, what is more, most white people (even those strongly in favor of assimilation of Indians into the dominant culture) are quick to charge a culturally rebellious Indian with the exploitation of his heritage. One thing conservative Indians and non-Indians seem to agree about is that good Indians are supposed to remain *pure*—which means that they are supposed to be static. So intense is the Western attitude toward Indian purity that sophisticated Indians are normally looked upon as not *really* being Indians. And so intense is the Indian regard for conformity that psychologists working with urbanized Native people are always pointing out the fact that their individuated patients suffer the same intense guilt toward their tribes that rebellious whites suffer in relation to their parents.

There is a crushing sociopsychological history among conservative Indians whose cultural tenacity somehow got confused with a sadly compromised grasp of their own heritage. A mixture of quasi-Christian morality, quasi-Indian activism, and a decline in their firsthand experience in Native American customs has resulted in a reactionary mentality that poses as traditionalism. Ironically, what Charles Eastman and Black Elk considered to be the "true spirit of the Indian" is immensely more vigorous, daring, and intelligent than what many rural Indians now regard as being "really Indian."* The compromises typical of middle Americans have left many Indians touched by a degraded and stereotypical "pow-wow" view of themselves.

The sociological problem appears to be that Indians had thousands of years to devise and evolve attitudes about themselves in relation to their self-contained cultures but have had pathetically little help and time to see themselves in relation to the culture that invaded their world. We therefore find Indians who recognize an excellent piece of pottery

---

*In fact Charles Eastman had the same disdain for reservation Indians (in comparison to Indians still living on the run) that today's reservation Indians express toward urban Native Americans who prefer the opportunities of the city to the extended family life of the reservation: "These people on the reservations are fat from the white man's food and foolish from his religion. They are only a shadow of what it really means to be an Indian." (*Indian Boyhood*, 1902)

with ease and then, unknowingly, fill it with plastic flowers. This distressing imbalance has persisted until very recently when nonassimilated Indians gained sufficient training in the skills of both the dominant and native cultures to possess an equal grasp of themselves and their values in both worlds.

In this way Indians have been discovering "themselves" for only a generation or two. Though urbanization and the influence of idiosyncratic Western mentality have undoubtedly prompted the growth of individuality among Indians, it is also possible that the singularity and personal charisma sought by most Plains Indians (in their vision quests, their triumphs in hunting and warring, etc.) would have been the basis for an evolution toward individuation among young Indians. In other words, it is very possible that Indians, at least Plains Indians, might be equally individualistic today even if they had persisted on this continent without the influence of Westerners. Of course, we shall never know.

Considering all of these possibilities, it should not be surprising that within the last decade several "schools" of idiosyncratic art have evolved out of the daring and contrariness of artists who side-stepped or openly defied tribal taboos. Such a school of art is the so-called Canadian Algonquin Legend Art that has taken shape recently in northern Ontario.

Its founder is a highly rebellious and antisocial fellow by the name of Norval Morrisseau who defied prohibitions against depicting events and characters from the legends of his people. As Bernard Cinader, an expert on the subject, wrote in 1977, "The first attempts of Morrisseau to paint the sacred legends of his people were fiercely resisted by those who guarded the secrets of the Medewiwin Society, but Morrisseau persisted and as he developed his own capacity as a painter, the opposition to his work gradually declined."

From this rebelliousness came a totally invented idiom of

Indian art which is almost entirely without debt in technique or media to Algonquin (Ojibwa-Odawa-Cree Indian) pictorial traditions. The figurations of Morrisseau's paintings possess a tentacled lineation slightly recalling the antennae which twine out of the shapes in the tapas of New Guinea. Except for its controversial legendary subject matter, Morrisseau's art has little relation to what we normally call North American Indian painting. There are fundamental aspects in his work of traditional Indian techniques, like outlining two-dimensional figures and filling the outlines with opaque, bright colors without modeling, but in the main his style is an invention as individualistic as anything produced by Matisse or Gauguin. In short, the Legend Art of Morrisseau represents a vital step in Indian individualism and announces a new era of Indian sensibility. Now Indians must find in their own way some form of individualism which suits their unique histories and cultures.

The Western world is in such social upheaval that it tends to want Indians like Morrisseau to stick with available stereotypes—a preconception that envisions Indians as mighty purveyors of static, unyielding traditionalism. But, clearly, being traditional and being reactionary are not the same things; and Indians must begin to change in their own way just as all people must, slowly or abruptly, slightly or greatly, quietly or rebelliously. It is difficult to think of an Indian artist who represents total rebellion better than Norval Morrisseau. He is truly the Indian Gauguin—not simply because both he and Gauguin were renegades and rebels, but because Morrisseau's rebellion was uniquely Indian—born out of his personal rejection of the constraints of the Indian world in which he grew up.

Both Gauguin and Morrisseau walked out on their very different but equally formal worlds—each for his own reason. Both artists had intense wanderlust—one seeking faraway romantic islands while the other sought the deep familiarity of nature itself; one searching externally while the other retreated within his own undiscovered natural world. And both of them produced a kind of art that angered and perplexed their very different audiences. Yet neither of them apologized for doing what he did nor attempted to mend the rift with society caused by his most singular and mystical sort of behavior. Each was absolutely atypical of the culture which produced him. And yet both were inevitable results of their social circumstances. Morrisseau is seen today as an eccentric in terms of the white world because he went off into the forest to live *within* nature; but much more importantly from the standpoint of this discussion, his real eccentricity from the Indian viewpoint is based on the fact that he thinks for himself and because he wants to be by himself and, especially, because he has broken taboos against the will of his tribe and doesn't give a damn what his people think about it. Gauguin's individuality was a process long coming in the Western world—the culmination of the romantic mood. Morrisseau's rebellion is uniquely Indian though it has been evolving in the Indian mentality for only a hundred years.

Throughout all this depiction of Morrisseau as a rebel, let us recall that he is not repudiating the validity of the Indian world or attempting to escape from it into some other world. He is not that kind of heretic. To the contrary, he is highly traditional (in his own way) and his works focus upon vital aspects of Indian culture. The difference between Morrisseau and Indian craftspeople of the past is that those like Morrisseau insist upon presenting whatever they personally envision as reality, and they do so with or without tribal consent, because the very core of their unprecedented motivation among Indians is to assert themselves in highly personal and idiosyncratic terms. The ultimate difference between Morrisseau and Gauguin is that those highly personal and idiosyncratic terms are distinctly Indian in Morrisseau's case while they are distinctly European in the case of Gauguin. Morrisseau never for a moment wanted to go "white" any more than Gauguin ever believed that he was really going "native."

Few contemporary Indians come to mind when we try to think of people who represent this kind of personal, assertive expressiveness and individualism. It is mainly among the painters that we find the daredevils, like Fritz Scholder and T. C. Cannon—who have been highly eccentric in their art and lives; each pursuing in a radically different way a totally personal vision even if it conflicted with and angered tribal authority, conservative Indian sensibility, and (let us not forget) those Anglo experts who always seem to know what Indians should be doing with their lives.

With the last decades of the twentieth century that fearsome quotation of Alfred North Whitehead concerning the responsibility of the future to be dangerous has come to apply for the first time to the world of Indians. Native people are producing intellectuals, artists, and militants who are appointing themselves to challenge and change what it means to be Indian. There is a strong lesson to be learned in this idiosyncratic thinking and art of contemporary Indians. If Native people admire tribal homogeneity, they automatically reject Morrisseau's assertiveness much as traditional whites repudiated the "created realities" of Gauguin, Kokashka, and de Kooning. Just as Western rebels bombarded the traditions of their own societies and often created new traditions that future generations rejected in their turn, so today's Indian rebelliousness is producing new definitions of what it means to be Indian in the twenty-first century and beyond.

For almost a decade those who pioneered the new world of Indian individualism have stood terrifyingly alone—dismissed equally by reactionary Indians and reactionary whites. But now their singularity is gradually ending, for a new breed of Indian intellectual is also emerging to champion the rebels and their creative causes. In the ideas and images of these rebellious Native Americans we clearly see American Indians re-creating themselves as Indian individuals. That is an essential part of the future of the primal mind.

10

THE ALTAMIRA
CONNECTION

> The traditional Native peoples hold the key to the reversal of the process in western civilization which holds the promise of unimaginable future suffering and destruction. Spiritualism is the highest form of political consciousness. And we, the Native Peoples of the Western Hemisphere, are among the world's surviving proprietors of that kind of consciousness. We are here to impart that message.
>
> —Position paper of the Six Nations presented at Geneva to the Non-Governmental Organizations of the United Nations, 1977

Observations of the decline of Western civilization are found everywhere in twentieth-century literature. Joseph Epes Brown has made an especially valuable equation that depicts this holocaust in terms of the positive potentials of primal peoples such as American Indians:

> We are faced today by what may be called a pervasive process on a global scale of detraditionalization or despiritualization. This process of detraditionalization and its manifestations has had an impact on the integrity of virtually all Native American traditions or lifeways. As this process of detraditionalization has proceeded its influence has demanded that the basic premises and orientations of our society be reevaluated. And in parallel manner we can perceive reevaluation of their own conditions by Native peoples themselves. This includes an assessment of their relationships to the materially dominant society. When sincere at-

tempt has been made by Native people to adjust to or accul-
turate within the dominant society, they have become
involved in a process of diminishing returns, or have
reached dead-ends with regard to acquiring a meaningful
quality of life.

What we are witnessing, according to Epes Brown, is the
struggle of both Indian and non-Indian to find answers to
their respective and dissimilar situations. Increasingly this
search has led to similar conclusions and attitudes—a variety
of attempts to regain contact with the roots of traditions
which, viewed by progressive thinkers as old-fashioned and
obsolete, have almost slipped into oblivion. Since Indian traditions are intrinsically bound to the very soil of the land
newly named America, unlike the alienating situation of
more recently transplanted Europeans, native persons have
a certain advantage in their quest for identity. Additionally,
the traditions and sacred ways of Native Americans have to
a large extent prevailed despite the overwhelming efforts to
obliterate them. For many urban as well as reservation Indians, that ancient tradition continues to provide a sense of alternative values which lends wholeness to the otherwise
shattered experience of twentieth-century life.

In this contemporary awareness of rootlessness, of gradual
detraditionalization, it is not surprising that non-Indians, especially young people, are turning to primal peoples and
their viable traditions for possible alternatives to the shaken
and collapsing values of their own societies. "The great
hope," Epes Brown states, "of this dual search on the part of
Indian and non-Indian is that a true and open dialogue may
be established through which neither will attempt to imitate
the other, but where each may ultimately regain and reaf-
firm the sacred dimensions of *their own* respective traditions."

In quoting Joseph Epes Brown and in my own praise of
the primal mind, I do not mean to buttress the current, vo-

guish viewpoint that only primal peoples can evolve true, undegenerate traditions and their pertinent rituals (rather than empty customs). To the contrary, I hope to open a vital question that the West has long avoided: "Who, and what precisely, are primal peoples?"

The word "primal" can easily become another of those gerrymandered terms of an ethnically self-conscious era, similar to the idealism and shortsightedness associated with such words as "feminist" and "black"; producing exclusivity out of a real rage rather than a realistic inclusivity out of a resolved hostility. Those whose experience has been destroyed are inevitably faced with an urge to destroy. It is no wonder that so-called minorities produce rhetoric that attempts to overcome adversity by destroying the experience of those who have destroyed their self-esteem. But, as we tragically came to understand during the 1970s, the process of hostility resolved nothing—not even hostility itself. Screams—no matter how primal—relieve symptoms; they don't cure social illnesses.

Therefore the use of a term like "the primal mind" should not be seen as the construction of a defense system that helps the pain by belittling and casting out those who caused it. The search for primal mentality is, to the contrary, an effort to praise our dissimilarities at the same time that it produces a consciousness among many of us (Indians and non-Indians) which is incalculably valuable, especially in the contemporary state of our world. That spiritual consciousness which I have called the primal mind is ageless and raceless, since it has been the means by which all eras and all races have articulated one of the grandest and most exceptional aspects of human possibility. It is not better than linear, Western mentality—though it may very well appear to be an improvement over the horrendous state the West is in today; it is simply an alternative to the Western way of thinking that has been chided, neglected, belittled, cast out, and abused for centuries—just as nonwhites, females, gays, and unpopular groups and individuals within white society itself have been abused.

The designation of primal mentality should not be used to deprecate those who do not possess it, but to elevate those who do possess it. It is a situation similar to the most radical feminists' stand, which appears to devote itself to the hatred of men and masculinity and the institutionalization of a power class in which women are not only self-reliant but self-sufficient like Amazons or black widow spiders. It seems to me that the real lesson of the feminists is that genderal role-playing is a hoax, that masculine and feminine (if we must retain such terms) describe not sex but personality; that the values of the so-called feminine mentality are found in males *and* females, depending on temperament and orientation. In short, feminine mentality like primal mentality is an alternative to the long-standing domination of male/Western mentality, not better but equally important, not exclusive to females or aboriginal people but also discovered in the psyche of the male and in the attitudes of urbane Western people. The research of sex researchers, the findings of those exploring the right/left brain specializations, and the myriad other discoveries in fields in which polarities are being destroyed or basically revaluated, should provide us with the capacity to tear down the defensive hostilities engendered by abuse and to begin to recognize that heritage, biological and cultural, is part of the marvelous endowment of humanity, and not the polarizing basis for renewing hostilities. "We are all related!" That is not an evocation of wishful thinking; but the most realistic reverberation of a long-standing Jungian image: *We all finally unite in one family tree, but what is a tree without its elaborately dissimilar branches?*

That we are all related does not make us all the same. Relationship does not require conformity, and the fact that one orientation or viewpoint is valuable does not preclude that all contrasting attitudes and positions are therefore erroneous and useless. Pluralism is a significant state of affairs for those who have been neglected; it is extremely bitter and difficult for those who have been long dominant. That's something we are going to have to learn to live with. We must learn to stop using public relations when dealing with the human spirit. We must stop helping people by trying to make them the same as we are, *whatever* that may be and no matter how ideally we are served by our unique identities. We must learn to praise dissimilarities just as we learned in the Renaissance to praise originality. *We must learn to use our minds to discover meaning rather than truth, and we must come to recognize that a variety of meanings and interpretations is what ultimately makes life truthful.*

The habits of linear thinking will not easily make room for the primal mind; not when this kind of thinking is the driving sensibility of aboriginal peoples and not when it is the inclination of scientists, philosophers, or anyone else in Western society who cannot claim rational exemption on the ground of being "artistic." But certain apparent ills in the West and certain catastrophic conditions may open the way to a few primal solutions which many scholars have pointed up: "The actual forces and events asserting themselves upon us at this present moment in our history," Joseph Epes Brown noted, "increasingly demand a backward look at progress so that such promises may be reexamined critically. Through such reexamination and possible reorientation, it may become possible for native American traditions to serve as a reminder of forgotten or neglected dimensions latent within the European American's own heritage."

From the polysynthetic metaphysic of nature envisioned by primal peoples, from a nature immediately experienced rather than dubiously abstracted, arises a premise that addresses itself with particular force to the root causes of many contemporary problems, especially to our present so-called ecological crisis. "It is perhaps this message of the sacred nature of the land," Epes Brown writes, "that today has been most responsible for forcing the Native American vision upon the mind and consciousness of the non-Indian."

The positive influences that the West might gain from the perspective of primal mentality are surely as vast, marvelous, and significant as the ideals and conceptions which have been produced by the West and which have gradually achieved almost global dominancy. Just as it now seems inevitable that Western authority will recede, it seems equally inevitable that primal thinking will assume an important role in the West. Many of the discussions in this book were aimed at producing an awareness of how thoroughly the primal mind has already influenced Western lifestyles and ideas. Making an unannounced and unwelcomed entrance through the widely neglected arts of the West, primal mentality has become the conscious and unconscious focus of the twentieth century. That is the ultimate irony of our era: those who have been most utterly defeated have become most influential. Another irony, of course, is that the most linear and material minds are not aware that history has relentlessly moved past them, putting their values in a new perspective which they cannot yet see.

It was said that when Rome fell the world would end. So utterly did the people of the vast empire believe in that adage that when Rome did, in fact, crumble and the Frankish domain became dominant in Western Europe, it was called the Holy Roman Empire in the mistaken belief that it was a continuation of the Roman Empire itself. In what is to me an entirely like manner, the West has not yet grasped its own demise and the subtle transformations which have made it something transitional and new. The West has not experienced itself in quite the way it does today since Plato articulated the supremacy of Logos and Paul heard the words of Christ with Platonic ears.

In the past when cultures perished, when Mycenae, Athens, and Rome dissipated, the land was overrun by so-called barbarians whose subjugation or persistent destruction had been a central aim of the declining civilizations. In this way, the great dominating cultures fade away and the outsiders, savages and barbarians, rise intermittently into a position of ideological and biological supremacy. From the brief rise of primal peoples comes a new culture that replaces the exhausted one. This is surely not a "law" of history, but it is certainly an apt description of much of what we know about recent historical events.

The value system that supports the highly unified social organism called civilization is apparently transient and perishable. Those who call themselves civilized have usually had a vision of their domain as ultimate and permanent. They think of their works as eternal, and they tend to consider themselves the sole survivors of a selective, evolutionary process. The "barbarians" on the other hand are thought to be obsolescent. Curiously, despite all of the world-shrinking technologies available to us at the end of the twentieth century, these supposedly obsolescent "primitives" are not only prevailing but multiplying, not just as producers of cultures and lifestyles but also as persistent sources of influences upon the entire interaction of human history. And, most interestingly, their impact, rather than being missionary, is largely unintentional.

So it seems that civilizations are impermanent. Yet the resources of primal peoples have not been depleted and have always managed to persist beyond the reach of the dominant cultures, which would surely subjugate or destroy them if they could do so. Unquestionably, the situation may change drastically in the future, but in the past it has been the resources of the world of primal peoples which have given impetus to the rise of human cultures. Thus the primal world has served as a self-perpetuating reservoir from which many human social cycles have evolved.

Though drastically simplified, the historical pattern seems to repeat itself: the Roman world strangled on its social incredibilities and its value system collapsed. The empire was overrun by Nordic hunters who, by Roman standards, were barely on the fringe of humanity. These barbarians helped to bring down the crumbling structures of Rome and from the wreckage they built Europe. In turn the Europeans eventually encountered the Africans, American Indians, and other primal peoples who became the new barbarians pitted against a new civilization.

In a remarkable article called *"Exploring the Mind of Ice Age Man,"* Alexander Marshack envisioned humanity as the persistent flowering of an ancient reality and not as a series of obsolescent and discontinued models. By my description of rising and fading civilizations I do not wish to imply that history has direction or self-contained values but merely that humanity possesses values and ideals as viable and real in the jungles, caves, and distant islands as those discovered in the grandest civilizations.

"What seems to be emerging from these new studies is a view of early man's way of thinking as being exceedingly complex and surprisingly modern," Marshack writes.

> In this culture of early *Homo sapiens* the real and the symbolic worlds were intertwined, and there was a continuity and sequence in man's ritual and ceremonial relationship to that world. Art, image, and notation were means of expressing that complex reality, of recognizing and participating in it. These are all human actions that require intelligence and a use of language. Moreover, they are aspects of man's early life that cannot be deduced merely from stone tools, for they are what anthropologists refer to as cognitive—that is, they

are a result of recognitions, abstractions, and solutions to problems, all of which take place in the brain. No more profound question exists than that of when and how this capacity began, and where, eventually, it will take us.

As early in this century as 1930, scholars such as Harry Elmer Barnes recognized a melding of primal and Western ideals, similar to the merging of Greek and Oriental civilizations during Hellenistic times, which brought about a brilliant synthesis that fused the two dominant pre-Christian cultures. "The best tribute to preliterary art is the fact that some of the most advanced school of painters and sculptors of the present day are going back to it for their inspiration. Primitivism in modern art is, consciously or not, a groping towards the aesthetics of precivilized man, an attempt to catch the pure vision found in his sculptured objects, wall paintings, and engravings."

The Stone Age murals found on the walls of caves in Spain and France constitute the fragile but significant continuum of human consciousness. Altamira is a reservoir of a spiritual mentality which, through eons of controversy and neglect, has survived to revivify our humanity when it seems in its moment of greatest peril. We are witnessing in this melding of primal and Western mentalities a synthesis as potentially brilliant as that fusion of Greek and Oriental ideals that produced the West. What lies in the future—if we survive the immense problems of our immediate technological dilemma—is the possibility of a world in which *every* aspect of human potentiality is given expression and in which the dominancy of just one kind of thinking may no longer be realistic or desirable. In this way, Altamira does not represent the past; nor is it a nostalgic vision of "better and simpler" times. Contrarily, Altamira is the bloom of that marvelous combination of recognitions, abstractions, and solutions to human problems which takes place in the brain and which illuminates the earliest culture of Homo sapiens and lights the way toward constant renewals of the ever-present immediacy of experience.

Altamira represents that sacredness of place and that perennial reality of the now which primal peoples have always understood as the first principle of their existence. It is a cognition that people of the West have rediscovered within their own ancestral cave. And so, in a curious way, contemporary Western people are rediscovering their past while primal peoples are discovering the present. They are emerging from the underworld into a new existence, but they are forever hidden from each other's view. It recalls the story of a Zuñi kachina who came out of the underworld attached back to back to a person from an alien world. Because they were obscured from each other's sight, it was taught that neither one was destined ever to see or to understand the other. "Yet," as Joseph Epes Brown comments when he recounts this story, "there is hope. It lies in the possibility that there may come a time for turning around, so that each may know who the other is and what the other might become."

That Zuñi parable reminds me of another fiction, *Through the Looking Glass* by Lewis Carroll, one of the first books to help me understand that my alienation was both precious and interchangeable with the experience of children of the dominant culture. Perhaps this dialogue between the Unicorn, Haigha, and Alice is an ideal closing for this summary of the life of the primal mind: for nothing has brought us as close to the original impulse of life as the wholly expressive assertions of innovators like Lewis Carroll, who are ready to sacrifice realism for the sake of a more powerful expression of the only rituals left to us—those which flow as art from whatever it is within us which we call "ourselves."

"What—is—this?" the Unicorn asked.
"This is a child!" Haigha replied eagerly, coming in front of Alice to introduce her.

"I always thought they were fabulous monsters!" said the Unicorn. "Is it alive?"

"It can talk," said Haigha solemnly.

The Unicorn looked dreamily at Alice, and said: "Talk, child."

Alice said: "Do you know, I always thought Unicorns were fabulous monsters, too. I never saw one alive before!"

"Well, now that we *have* seen each other," said the Unicorn, "if you'll believe in me, I'll believe in you. Is that a bargain?"

SELECTIVE
BIBLIOGRAPHY

Arendt, Hannah. *The Life of the Mind: Volume One: Thinking*. New York: Harcourt Brace Jovanovich, 1971.
————. *The Life of the Mind: Volume Two: Willing*. New York: Harcourt Brace Jovanovich, 1978.
Ashbery, John. "Picasso." *New York* magazine, May 12, 1980.
Astrov, Margot, ed. *American Indian Prose and Poetry: An Anthology*. New York: Capricorn Books, 1946.
Bandelier, Adolph. *The Southwestern Journals, 1880–1888*. Albuquerque: University of New Mexico Press, 1966.
Barnes, Harry Elmer. *An Intellectual and Cultural History of the Western World*. New York: Reynal & Hitchcock, 1941.
BBC. *The Institutions of Primitive Society: A Series of Broadcast Talks*. Oxford: Basil Blackwell, 1967.
Bell, Clive. *Art*. New York: Capricorn Books, 1958.
Berkhofer, Jr., Robert F. *The White Man's Indian: Images of the American Indian from Columbus to the Present*. New York: Alfred A. Knopf, 1978.
Berndt, Catherine H., and Ronald M. Berndt. *The Barbarians: An Anthropological View*. Middlesex, England: Penguin Books, 1971.
Black Elk. *See* John G. Neihardt.
Boas, Franz. *The Mind of Primitive Man*. New York: The Free Press, 1965.
Brasser, Ted. "Wolf Collar: The Shaman As Artist." In *Stones, Bones and Skin*, edited by Ann Trueblood Brodzky. Toronto: Society for Art Publications, 1977.
Brodzky, Ann Trueblood, ed. *Stones, Bones and Skin: Ritual and Shamanic Art*. An Arts Canada Book. Toronto: Society for Art Publications, 1977.
Brosses, Charles de. *Du Culte des dieux fetiches*. Paris, 1760.
Brown, Joseph Epes. *See* Walter Holden Capps.
Burke, Kenneth. *Psychology and Form*. New York: Macmillan Co., 1947.

Busignani, Alberto. *Pollock.* Middlesex: Hamlyn Publishing Group, 1971.

Campbell, Joseph. *The Masks of God: Occidental Mythology.* New York: The Viking Press, 1964.

———. *The Masks of God: Primitive Mythology.* New York: The Viking Press, 1970.

Capps, Walter Holden, ed. *Seeing with a Native Eye: Essays on Native American Religion.* New York: Harper & Row, 1976.

Carpenter, Edmund. "Silent Music and Invisible Art." *Natural History Magazine,* May 1978, pp. 90–99.

Carroll, Lewis. *Through the Looking Glass.* New York: Vintage Books, 1976 (original publication, 1872).

Carroll, Peter N., and David W. Noble. *The Free and the Unfree: A New History of the United States.* New York: Penguin Books, 1977.

Cassirer, Ernst. *An Essay on Man: An Introduction to a Philosophy of Human Culture.* New Haven: Yale University Press, 1944.

———. *Language and Myth.* New York: Dover Publications, 1946.

Chapman, Abraham, ed. *Literature of the American Indians: Views and Interpretations.* New York: New American Library, 1975.

Cinader, Bernard. "Tradition and Aspiration in Contemporary Canadian Indian Art." In *Contemporary Indian Art.* Ontario: Trent University Press, 1977.

Condorcet, Marie Jean Antoine Nicolas de Caritat. *Sketch for a Historical Picture of the Progress of the Human Mind.* London: Weidenfeld and Nicolson, 1955 (original publication, 1795).

Daiches, David. *The Novel and the Modern World.* Chicago: University of Chicago Press, 1960.

Degler, Carl N. "Indians and Other Americans." *Commentary Magazine,* November 1972, pp. 68–72.

Deloria, Jr., Vine. *We Talk, You Listen: New Tribes, New Turf.* New York: Macmillan Co., 1970.

———. *God Is Red.* New York: Grosset & Dunlap, 1973.

Deregowski, Jan B. "Pictorial Perception and Culture." *Scientific American,* November 1972.

De Waal Malefijt, Annemarie. *Images of Man: A History of Anthropological Thought.* New York: Alfred A. Knopf, 1974.

Díaz del Castillo, Bernal. *The Conquest of New Spain.* Translated by J. M. Cohen. London: Penguin Classics, 1963.

Dlugoszewski, Lucia. "What Is Sound to Music?" *Main Currents in Modern Thought,* September–October 1973, pp. 3–11.

Driver, Harold E. *Indians of North America.* Chicago: University of Chicago Press, 1961.

Dufrenne, Mikel. *The Phenomenology of Aesthetic Experience.* Evanston, Ill.: Northwestern University Press, 1973.

Eastman, Charles A. *Indian Boyhood.* Greenwich, Ct.: A Fawcett Premier Book, 1972 (original publication, 1902).

Edinger, Edward F. *Philosophical Papers*. In *Quadrant*, vol. 11, no. 2, Winter 1978.

Eiseley, Loren. *The Firmament of Time*. New York: Atheneum Publishers, 1975.

Eliot, T. S. *Selected Essays*. London: Faber & Faber, 1932.

Farb, Peter. *Man's Rise to Civilization: The Cultural Ascent of the Indians of North America*. New York: Bantam Books, 1978.

Ferguson, Adam. Quoted in John W. Burrow, *Evolution and Society*. Cambridge: Cambridge University Press, 1966.

Fiedler, Leslie A. *Love and Death in the American Novel*. New York: Stein & Day, 1960.

————. *The Return of the Vanishing American*. New York: Stein & Day, 1968.

Freedman, Daniel G. *Human Sociobiology*. New York: The Free Press, 1979.

————. "Ethnic Differences in Babies." *Human Nature*, January 1979, pp. 36–43.

Gadamer, Hans-Georg. *Philosophical Hermeneutics*. Berkeley: University of California Press, 1976.

Gallagher D. P. *Modern Latin American Literature*. Oxford: Oxford University Press, 1973.

Grimes, Ronald L. *Symbol and Conquest: Public Ritual and Drama in Santa Fe, New Mexico*. Ithaca: Cornell University Press, 1976.

Halifax, Joan. *Shamanic Voices: A Survey of Visionary Narratives*. New York: E. P. Dutton, 1979.

Hanke, Lewis. *Aristotle and the American Indians: A Study in Race Prejudice in the Modern World*. Bloomington: Indiana University Press, 1975.

Harris, Marvin. *Cows, Pigs, Wars and Witches: The Riddles of Culture*. New York: Vintage Books, 1974.

————. *Cannibals and Kings: The Origins of Cultures*. New York: Random House, 1977.

Harrison, Jane Ellen. *Epilegomena to the Study of Greek Religion* and *THEMIS: A Study of the Social Origins of Greek Religion*. New Hyde Park, N.Y.: University Books, 1962.

Herskovits, Melville J. *Cultural Relativism: Perspectives in Cultural Pluralism*. New York: Random House, 1972.

Hess, Hans. *How Pictures Mean*. New York: Pantheon Books, 1974.

Highwater, Jamake. Fodor's *Indian America*. New York: David McKay Co., 1975.

————. *Song from the Earth: American Indian Painting*. Boston: New York Graphic Society, 1976.

————. *ANPAO: An American Indian Odyssey*. New York: J. B. Lippincott, 1977.

————. *Ritual of the Wind: North American Indian Ceremonies, Music, and Dances*. New York: The Viking Press, 1977.

216   SELECTIVE BIBLIOGRAPHY

————. *Many Smokes, Many Moons: A Chronology of American Indian History through Indian Art.* New York: J. B. Lippincott, 1978.
————. *Dance: Rituals of Experience.* New York: A & W Publishers, 1978.
Hobson, Geary, ed. *The Remembered Earth: An Anthology of Contemporary Native American Literature.* Albuquerque, N.M.: Red Earth Press, 1979.
Hughes, J. Donald. "Forest Indians: The Holy Occupation." *Environmental Review,* February 1977, pp. 2–13.
Husserl, Edmund. *The Crisis of European Man.* New York: Harper Torchbooks, 1965.
Jacobsen, Thorkild. *The Treasures of Darkness: A History of Mesopotamian Religion.* New Haven: Yale University Press, 1976.
Jacobson, Angeline, comp. *Contemporary Native American Literature: A Selected and Partially Annotated Bibliography.* Metuchen: Scarecrow Press, 1977.
Johnson, Lusita B., and Stephen Proskauer, M.D. "Hysterical Psychosis in a Pre-Pubescent Navajo Girl." *Journal of the American Academy of Child Psychiatry,* New Haven: Yale University Press, 1974.
Jung, Carl G. *Psychological Reflections: A New Anthology of His Writings, 1905–1961.* Princeton: Princeton University Press, 1953.
Kandinsky, Wassily. *Concerning the Spiritual in Art.* Translated by M. T. Sadler. New York: Dover Publications, 1977.
Katz, Jonathan. *Gay American History: Lesbians and Gay Men in the U.S.A.* A documentary. New York: Thomas Y. Crowell, 1976.
Kurz, Rudolph Friederich. *Journal.* Washington, D.C.: Smithsonian Institution, 1937.
La Barre, Weston. *The Human Animal.* Chicago: University of Chicago Press, 1954.
————. *The Peyote Cult.* New York: Schocken Books, 1969.
————. *The Ghost Dance: Origins of Religion.* London: George Allen and Unwin, 1970.
Langer, Susanne K. *Philosophy in a New Key: A Study in the Symbolism of Reason, Rite, and Art.* Cambridge: Harvard University Press, 1942.
————. *Problems of Art: Ten Philosophical Lectures.* New York: Charles Scribner's Sons, 1957.
Las Casas, Bartolome de. Quoted in Lewis Hanke, *The First Social Experiments in America.* Cambridge: Harvard University Press, 1935.
Lawrence, D. H. *The Vast Old Religion of Taos,* 1936. Quoted in *The Intelligent Heart* by Harry T. Moore. London: Penguin Books, 1954.
Lee, Dorothy. *Freedom and Culture.* Homewood, Ill.: Prentice-Hall, 1959.
Leon-Portilla, Miguel. *The Broken Spears.* Aztec Accounts of the Conquest of Mexico. Translated by Lysander Kemp. New York: Beacon Press, 1962.
Levin, Harry. *James Joyce.* New York: New Directions, 1941.

Lévi-Strauss, Claude. *The Savage Mind*. Chicago: University of Chicago Press, 1966.

Lévy-Brühl, Lucien. *The "Soul" of the Primitive*. Chicago: Henry Regnery Co., 1966.

Lorca, Federico García. *Poems*. Translated by Stephen Spender and J. L. Gili. New York: Oxford University Press, 1939.

Lowie, Robert H. *Primitive Society*. New York: Liveright, 1947.

———. *Primitive Religion*. New York: Liveright, 1948.

Lucie-Smith, Edward. *Art Now: From Abstract Expressionism to Superrealism*. New York: William Morrow and Co., 1977.

Machado-Ruiz, Antonio. Quoted in Jean Franco, *An Introduction to Spanish-American Literature*. Cambridge: Cambridge University Press, 1969.

McNickle, D'Arcy. *The Surrounded*. Albuquerque: University of New Mexico Press, 1936.

Mann, Thomas. *The Magic Mountain*. New York: Alfred A. Knopf, 1927.

Marcuse, Herbert. *Eros and Civilization*. Boston: Beacon Press, 1955.

Marshack, Alexander. "Exploring the Mind of Ice Age Man." *National Geographic*, January 1975, pp. 65–89.

Martin, John. *America Dancing*. New York: Dance Horizons, 1968.

Matthews, Washington. *Navajo Legends*. New York: American Folklore Society, 1897.

Mellers, Wilfred. *Caliban Reborn: Renewal in Twentieth-Century Music*. New York: Harper & Row, 1967.

Merleau-Ponty, Maurice. *Sense and Non-Sense*. Evanston, Ill.: Northwestern University Press, 1964a.

———. *Signs*. Evanston, Ill.: Northwestern University Press, 1964b.

———. *The Primacy of Perception: And Other Essays on Phenomenological Psychology, the Philosophy of Art History and Politics*. Evanston, Ill.: Northwestern University Press, 1964c.

———. *Eye and Mind*. Evanston, Ill.: Northwestern University Press, 1964d.

Momaday, N. Scott. *House Made of Dawn*. Middlesex, England; Penguin Books, 1966.

———. *The Way to Rainy Mountain*. New York: Ballantine Books, 1969.

———. *The Names: A Memoir*. New York: Harper & Row, 1976.

Moreux, Serge. *Béla Bartók*. New York: Vienna House, 1974.

Morgan, Barbara. Quoted in *Growth of Dance in America*, vol. 13, no. 2. Madison: University of Wisconsin, 1976.

Morton, Samuel George. *Crania Americana*. Philadelphia: J. Penington, 1839.

Muller, Herbert J. *The Uses of the Past: Profiles of Former Societies*. New York: Oxford University Press, 1957.

Neihardt, John G. *Black Elk Speaks*. London: Sphere Books, 1974.

Niatum, Duane, ed. *Carriers of the Dream Wheel: Contemporary Native American Poetry*. New York: Harper & Row, 1975.

Noel, Daniel, ed. *Seeing Castaneda: Reactions to the "Don Juan" Writings of Carlos Castaneda*. New York: G. P. Putnam's Sons, 1976.

Northrop, F.S.C. *Man, Nature and God: A Quest for Life's Meaning*. New York: Pocket Books, 1962.

―――. *The Meeting of East and West*. New York: Collier Books, 1966.

Ornstein, Robert E. *The Psychology of Consciousness*. New York: Penguin Books, 1975.

Ortiz, Alfonso. *The Tewa World: Space, Time, Being, and Becoming in a Pueblo Society*. Chicago: University of Chicago Press, 1969.

Osborne, Harold. *Aesthetics and Art Theory: An Historical Introduction*. New York: E. P. Dutton and Co., 1970.

Paz, Octavio. *The Labyrinth of Solitude*. London: Allen Lane, Penguin Press, 1967.

―――. *The Other Mexico: Critique of the Pyramid*. New York: Grove Press, 1972.

Penfield, Wilder. *The Mystery of the Mind: A Critical Study of Consciousness and the Human Brain*. Princeton: Princeton University Press, 1975.

Philipson, Morris. *Aesthetics Today*. Cleveland, Ohio: Meridian Books, 1961.

Popul Vuh. English version by Delia Goetz and Sylvanus G. Morley, from the translation by Adrian Recinos. Norman: University of Oklahoma Press, 1950.

Prescott, William H. *The Conquest of Mexico*. New York: Modern Library, 1943 (original publication, 1843).

Qoyawayma, Polingaysi (Elizabeth Q. White), as told to Vada F. Carlson. *No Turning Back: A true account of a Hopi Indian girl's struggle to bridge the gap between the world of her people and the world of the white man*. Albuquerque: University of New Mexico Press, 1964.

Radin, Paul. *Primitive Man As Philosopher*. New York: Dover Publications, 1952.

―――. *Primitive Religion: Its Nature and Origin*. New York: Dover Publications, 1957.

―――. *The World of Primitive Man*. New York: E. P. Dutton and Co., 1971.

Rahv, Philip. *Image and Idea*, containing "Notes on the Decline of Naturalism." New York: New Directions, 1949.

Read, Herbert. *The Philosophy of Modern Art*. New York: Horizon Press, 1953.

―――. *Icon and Idea: The Function of Art in the Development of Human Consciousness*. New York: Schocken Books, 1965.

―――. *Henry Moore: A Study of His Life and Work*. New York: Frederick A. Praeger, 1965.

―――. *Art and Society*. New York: Schocken Books, 1966.

Robertson, Bryan. Quoted in Busignani.

Rodin, Auguste. Quoted in *The Primacy of Perception. See* Maurice Merleau-Ponty.

Rosen, Kenneth, ed. *The Man to Send Rain Clouds: Contemporary Stories by American Indians.* New York: Vintage Books, 1974.

Rudofsky, Bernard. *Architecture Without Architects: A Short Introduction to Non-Pedigreed Architecture.* Garden City, N.Y.: Doubleday and Co., 1964.

Sagan, Carl. *The Dragons of Eden: Speculations on the Evolution of Human Intelligence.* New York: Random House, 1977.

Sahagun, Bernardino de. *Historia general de las casas de Nueva Espana.* English-Nahuatl ed. Dibble and Anderson, eds. Part III. Albuquerque, N.M.: School of American Research and University of Utah Press, 1975.

Schiller, Herbert, I. *Communication and Cultural Domination.* White Plains: M. E. Sharpe, 1976.

Scully, Vincent. *Pueblo Mountain, Village, Dance.* New York: The Viking Press, 1972.

Sepulveda, Juan Gines de. *Texts and Studies,* vol 5. Princeton: Princeton University Press, 1916.

Silko, Leslie Marmon. *Ceremony: A Novel.* New York: The Viking Press, 1977.

Simmons, Leo W., ed. *Sun Chief: The Autobiography of a Hopi Indian.* New Haven: Yale University Press, 1942.

Speck, Frank G., and Leonard Broom. *Cherokee Dance and Drama.* Berkeley: University of California Press, 1951.

Stent, Gunther S. *Paradoxes of Progress.* San Francisco: W. H. Freeman and Co., 1924.

Stevens, Wallace. "The Noble Rider and the Sound of Words." In *The Language of Poetry.* Edited by Allen Tate. Princeton: Princeton University Press, 1942.

Stevenson, Matilda Coxe. *The Zuñi Indians.* Twenty-third Annual Report, U.S. Bureau of American Ethnology: 1901–1902. Washington, D.C.: Smithsonian Institution, 1904.

Storm, Hyemeyohsts. *Seven Arrows.* New York: Harper & Row, 1972.

Stravinsky, Igor. Quoted in *Stravinsky in Pictures and Documents,* by Vera Stravinsky and Robert Craft. New York: Simon and Schuster, 1978.

Strete, Craig Kee. *Paint Your Face on a Drowning in the River.* New York: Greenwillow Books, 1978.

Tax, Sol, Ed. *Anthropology Today: Selections.* Chicago: University of Chicago Press, 1962.

Taylor, Michael. "Faces and Voices." *Moccasins on Pavement.* Denver: Denver Museum of Natural History, 1979.

Tedlock, Dennis, and Barbara Tedlock, eds. *Teachings from the American Earth: Indian Religion and Philosophy.* New York: Liveright, 1975.

Thomas, Lewis. *The Medusa and the Snail*. New York: The Viking Press, 1979.

Time-Life Books. *The Old West: The Indians*. New York: Time-Life Books. 1973.

Trilling, Lionel. *The Liberal Imagination*. New York: Charles Scribner's Sons, 1950.

Underhill, Ruth M. *Red Man's Religion: Beliefs and Practices of the Indians North of Mexico*. Chicago: University of Chicago Press, 1965.

Vico, Giambattista. *The New Science of Giambattista Vico*. Garden City, N.Y.: Doubleday, 1961 (original publication, 1725).

Von Grunebaum, G. E., and Roger Caillois. *The Dream and Human Societies*. Berkeley: University of California Press, 1966.

Vonnegut, Jr., Kurt. Interview in *The New Fiction*, by Joe David Bellamy. Urbana: University of Illinois Press, 1974.

Wagner, Richard. *Opera and Drama*. In *Collected Prose Works*. London, 1892–99. (*Opera and Drama* originally published 1852 in Leipzig.)

Welch, James. *Riding the Earthboy 40: Poems*. New York: Harper & Row, 1971.

————. *Winter in the Blood: A Novel*. New York: Harper & Row, 1974.

Werner, Heinz. *Comparative Psychology of Mental Development*. New York: Harper & Row, 1940.

Whitehead, Alfred North. *Science and the Modern World*. New York: The Free Press, 1925.

Whorf, Benjamin Lee. *Language, Thought, and Reality*. Cambridge, Mass.: M.I.T. Press, 1956.

Whyte, Lancelot Law. *The Next Development in Man*. New York: Henry Holt and Co., 1948.

Williamson, Ray. "Native Americans Were Continent's First Astronomers." *The Smithsonian*, October 1978, pp. 78–85.

Witherspoon, Gary. *Language and Art in the Navajo Universe*. Ann Arbor: University of Michigan Press, 1977.

Wood, Nancy. *The Man Who Gave Thunder to the Earth: A Taos Way of Seeing and Understanding*. Garden City, N.Y.: Doubleday and Co., 1976.

Zukav, Gary. *The Dancing Wu Li Masters, An Overview of the New Physics*. New York: William Morrow, 1979.

NAME AND SOURCE INDEX

221

SUBJECT INDEX

Aborigines, 25, 89, 154
Abstract Expressionism, 121
acculturation, cultural assimilation
  vs., xi, 11–12
actors, social role of, 178, 179
aerial perspective, 119
aesthetic dimension, 155
African art, 46–47, 51, 154
Algonquins, 83
  Legend Art of, 197–98
alienation:
  dance and, 151
  harmony as defense against, 193,
    194
  importance of, xiv–xv
  individualism and, 171, 172
  as metaphor, xiv–xv, 15, 193–201
alphabetical writing, 72
Altamira, cave art, 15–16, 46, 210–11
Alvin Ailey Company, 140
ambiguity, 65–66, 68
  primal vs. Western views on, 144
  ritual and, 44, 144, 147
American School, 34
anarchy, Western fear of, 180
Anasazi, 129
'a'ne himu ("a mighty something"),
  67
animals, 73–74
  dance as influence on, 141, 142
  evolution and, 18–19, 22, 24, 35
  images of, 37, 58, 59, 61, 83, 136
  unconscious compared to, 60
anthropology, 18, 20–21, 25, 28,
  40–41

antisocial behavior, 195
  of sacred clowns, 174–81
  Western views on, 174, 178–79
Apache, sacred clowns as viewed by,
  174
Apache "fiddle," 163
apes, evolution of, 18–19
archaeology, 18, 37–38
archetypes, 10, 51, 118
architecture, 37, 48, 122–27
  astronomical motion incorporated
    in, 128–30
  images used for, 78–79, 85
  kivas as, 122, 124–26
  Medicine Wheels as, 126–27, 130
  tipis as, 78–79, 85, 122
art, aesthetics:
  African, 46–47, 51, 154
  Asian, 45–46, 49, 162, 164, 165
  birth of "the self" in, 194–95
  as bridge to "the other," 13–16
  Byzantine, 62
  Christian influences on, 133–34,
    135, 139, 149, 153, 154
  conceptualizing and specialization
    of, 55, 141, 148–49
  differences in world views re-
    vealed in, 6–7, 56–58, 114–17
  essences vs. appearances in, 58–59,
    61, 87–88, 118
  facts vs. aesthetic component in,
    13–14, 15, 16
  in Freudian theory, 60
  Gothic, 59, 62
  Greek, 43, 62, 124, 153, 195